GW00658187

Conter

BIG HANDICAP WINNERS

by
Patrick Kilgallon

ISBN: 1-901100-48-0

BIG HANDICAP WINNERS

Chapter 1: Why bet in big handicaps?

WHAT is a big handicap? Such is the impecunious state of British racing that in terms of prize money any race which pays over £30,000 to the winner is a big handicap. In Hong Kong, there are big handicaps every racing day, but in Britain on average one every racing week. There are also some less well-rewarded races, such as those at the major meetings (Goodwood July, Doncaster St Leger) or at two courses (Newmarket, The Curragh), which are always so strongly competed for that they also fall into the category of big handicaps.

Some backers avoid these handicaps, because they think that the results are unpredictable, or that the big prizes tempt trainers to 'lay out' a 'dark horse' with no public form to win both a big prize and a big bet. If it is difficult enough to find winners in handicaps, surely it is impossible to find winners in the big handicaps? A quick glance at the form book seems to support this view, with enough examples to deter anyone from taking an interest in such races. Look at the Royal Hunt Cup in the 1990s, with winners at 50-1, 25-1, 20-1, 20-1, 25-1, 16-1, and 20-1. Or, even more unpromisingly, the shock winners of the Wokingham: 16-1, 14-1, 33-1, 20-1, 14-1, 33-1, 25-1, 16-1, and 14-1. These long-priced winners, were often unfancied not only by journalists and form students, as they had shown little ability in public, but also by their owners and trainers. With the aid of a pin, you might have picked some of these winners...but, predictable? as about as predictable as a Railtrack timetable.

I quite agree that some big handicaps do generate a string of 'shocks' welcomed only by the bookmakers. If these races were human beings, they would be covered in oozing splotches, ringing a bell, and shouting 'unclean'. Avoid them under all circumstances. But it is illogical to conclude that all big handicaps belong to this category and, as you will see, the races which should always be avoided can be clearly identified. At the other extreme, some big handicaps are worth betting on almost every year. In all, each year there are about 50 'big handicaps', offering on average 12 bets.

For the careful backer, big handicaps have a number of advantages over ordinary handicaps. They fall under these headings: form reliability; trend evidence; trainer predictability; information availability; and betting advantage.

Form reliability. Big handicaps are usually contested by large fields (20 runners or more). I am a great believer in the saying 'the bigger the field the bigger the certainty'. By 'certainty' I do not mean 'favourite' but 'form horse (s). Form works out more reliably in big handicaps with large fields than in any other kind of race.

The early stages of races with small fields (ten runners or fewer) are often run at snail speed. The strong gallopers, held up for a late run, do not set a pace to sap the reserves of their stamina-doubtful rivals and in the final stages, the race develops into a sprint which these weaker horses can win. When a result is otherwise inexplicable, the cause is usually a false pace. And have you ever seen a large-field handicap follow the early crawl/late scramble pattern? The main objection to 'the bigger the field' maxim, is that there are much greater possibilities of interference, leading to numerous 'hard luck' stories. Interference does happen, but I am very sceptical about the 'X would have won if only he had had a clear run in the final furlong.' Subsequent results usually justify my scepticism, as the 'unlucky loser' still cannot win with the clearest of runs to the winning post. Paradoxically, interference can make a horse's performance seem better and not worse than it really was, i.e. if the horse does not have quite enough speed to dash for the line, this may not be evident if he is checked.

In any case interference is much more likely to happen at some courses (for example, Chester, where the runners are continually on the turn round a tight circuit) than others. The wide straight courses with a long run-in (for example, Doncaster, Goodwood and York) and (better still) an uphill finish (Cheltenham, Newmarket, The Curragh) can easily accommodate large fields. A strong pace means that in the final stages the tired horses begin to roll, opening up gaps for the fitter competitors, so that there is little danger of being shut in.

By a fortunate coincidence nearly all the big handicaps are run at these testing courses. If they were all run at courses with a downhill section on the final run in (Epsom) or with tight bends (Chester), then it would be far more difficult to find winners.

Not only does form work out well in big handicaps, but such races also provide reliable lines of form for the future. No better form test can be devised than a competitive race, with a strong gallop throughout, and the result still in doubt until the final stages. By contrast, many non-handicaps, including those with valuable prizes, are run at a muddling pace followed by a two furlongs sprint to the line. In the post-race appraisals, the phrases 'if only', 'might have', 'would have' occur too frequently to reassure the reader that he can rely on the form show in such races.

Trend evidence. In addition to studying the form of today's race you can (and must) examine the trends shown in previous years. Almost all the races analysed in this book have been run for at least 20 years, long enough for patterns to be established. The record can then be inspected for both the statistical trends (in terms of age, weight and rating) and the form trends (what kind of races are the right preparation).

The big handicap programme has remained fairly stable over the last 30 years. The two major changes which have taken place over the last decade, the decline in the importance of the Flat handicaps run at the 'Home Counties' courses (Epsom, Kempton, Newbury and Sandown), and the lack of valuable 10f handicaps, are marginal to the programme as a whole. By contrast, the entire focus of the non-handicap programme has changed quite quickly over the last twenty years. The season has shifted towards the autumn and the races abroad, so that the English classics, particularly the two Guineas, are no longer so very important.

The trend evidence has to be analysed from two points of view: statistical (age, rating and, for certain types of races, weight) and form (in handicaps). 'Ten-Year-Trends' compiled by Craig Thake, which appears in Racing Post, is invaluable for statistics, but does not always give the historical record of form. Andrew Ayres's book, Trendsetters Review for the Flat (A statistical guide to 110 major races) (Raceform 2000) pays more attention to form, but it does not give as much detailed information as you will find in chapter 3 of this book. Trainer predictability. The big handicaps are usually won by the leading trainers. This statement does not apply to quite the same extent in National Hunt racing, but their overall dominance is unquestionable. These trainers usually follow a tried and well tested route to the big prizes, whereas their approach to the ordinary handicaps is much less predictable. Their methods can be studied over several years, and given that the handicap programme is so stable, it makes sense for them to find a winning formula early in their careers and to apply it without variation.

Trainers' habits do not change over time, except when they concentrate on particular types of races. For example, in the 1970s and 1980s Sir Michael Stoute won the big sprint handicaps fairly often, but in the last decade he has concentrated on middle-distance horses. God is indeed on the side of the big racing battalions. A small stable will find it very difficult to estimate the ability of a promising novice, since it is likely that there is no competition within the yard. A big stable has not only several hopefuls, but usually houses recent winners against which their promise can be tested. Testing against the clock is not a satisfactory substitute for a gallop against experienced animals.

Trainers seem to start before they are 30 and to carry on for 30 years, a level of continuity very unusual in any other sport. For example, look at the starting date of some of racing's current training stars: I A Balding (1964), J L Dunlop (1966), B W Hills (1969), Sir Michael Stoute (1972), and, a relative newcomer, L Cumani (1976).

New trainers emerge very quickly. Perhaps this is because the higher class trainers spend several years as an assistant to an already established trainer, so that when they set up on their own, they already have considerable experience and it soon becomes clear whether they have the kind of ability we are looking for. They may not immediately be able to employ their talents in the higher class handicaps, but their potential for doing so is soon apparent. It may be easier for new trainers to make an impact in National Hunt racing because the more dispersed pattern of ownership compared to the Flat gives newcomers more of a chance. Certainly, the year at the races reviewed in Chapter 6 saw the emergence of two steeplechase trainers at the highest level (Ferdy Murphy and J J O'Neill), but none in Flat racing. By concentrating on the top stables, you do not even have to think about jockeys, as they always employ the leading riders. These stables also tend to make clever use of apprentices, so that you can trust their judgement when they employ the most inexperienced apprentices, the seven pounds claimers. Conversely, the booking of a leading jockey by a small stable can send a confusing message: does it have any significance or is the jockey simply making up his rides for that day? Information availability. Not all of the leading trainers have the mentality of a spin doctor when it comes to giving out information. Some trainers readily give an honest opinion about their runners' preferences for going and distance, or, even better, will candidly state that they have doubts about a runner's chance. The latter kind of information is worth its weight in platinum, especially when, as happens surprisingly often, it is ignored by racegoers even to the point of making the runner a short-priced favourite. Then you know that you can discount the horse, and that the price of your selection may be artificially boosted.

Naturally enough, the racing press and TV focus on the big handicaps to the exclusion of the lesser prizes.There is one rather depressing feature of the press coverage of these races. If the newspapers carry a feature about a small stable which appears to have a live chance in a big handicap, then, sadly, this seems to have the effect of tying the horse's feet together. This is no reflection on the journalists (who have to find a story) or the stables (who are quite sincere about their chances and hope that a winner in a will catapult them into a bigger league). The betting advantage. The betting advantage in big handicaps is twofold. In minor handicaps the strength of the form candidates and the weakness of the rest of the field are equally obvious. The market usually focusses on the form horses, leading to short prices. In big handicaps quite a number of horses can be given a chance of sorts (even if, as our analysis in chapters 3 and 4 will show that they have a negligible chance of winning), so that the market is not so focussed on one or two runners, and the prices are not so short.

The second advantage is that, much more than any other type of race, big handicaps are likely to generate 'false-priced favourites', i.e. a favourite which you can be very confident will lose. In the distorted betting market in these races, you can find very good value odds against your selection (see chapter 5 for a detailed account of 'false-priced favourites').

However, big handicaps do suffer from one disadvantage. The backer must be patient, until the right form combination is locked into place. For example, to have a good chance of winning the Ayr Gold Cup, a horse must have shown good form at certain specified courses, and the race must be run on good or good to firm going. In six years out of ten, the going is soft; and in the remaining four years, runners with the right form credentials may only appear two or three times. So, at most, you only have a three in ten chance of making a reasonable selection.

Even with all these advantages, the reader may still be asking the question: in the highly competitive world of big handicaps, does the ordinary backer with no access to inside information have any competitive edge? Against the two other main groups, the bookmakers and journalists, which have an interest in predicting the results, the ordinary backer seems to be at a complete disadvantage. How can s/he compete with their financial backing and access to information? The answer was given by a very astute bookmaker, Victor

Chandler, when he said that the only advantage the ordinary punter has is that he doesn't have to bet in every race. The bookmakers know which races are particularly profitable to them (and often these are the races they subsidise), but they also know that they will have losing races. However much they may try to shorten the prices on these races, they still cannot completely avoid trading. The journalist is obliged to comment on every race, whether s/he feels at all confident about his selections or not. How long would it be before a journalist who wrote a headline such as 'The Tripleprint handicap is tricky - don't bet today' would be handed his P45?

My approach to big handicaps is to study form and not ignore the obvious. In a big handicap, a 'form' horse is one which has won recently in good style over the distance; has shown in the past that he can act on the going; and fits the form and statistical trends. Although the credentials of such horses are usually self-evident, many punters not only ignore the obvious, but go a long way out of their way to flout the obvious. I think that this is because they not only want to back winners, but want to back 'clever' winners. Far from being the flamboyant figures of punters' imaginations, many professional backers are, in their preference for 'obvious' selections, extremely dull fellows indeed. Although the approach set out in this book follows the watchword 'keep it obvious', I accept that there are at least two other ways to be successful in backing the winners of big handicaps. They involve looking for 'dark horses' prepared for this race by a leading trainer, or for 'possible' winners which have won over a slightly different distance or have run promisingly without winning.

Although this book favours the form horse, I have given as much information as I have been able to find about 'dark' horses. Some trainers have a consistent record in certain races with this type of horse, and they should never be ignored. The 'possible' winner type is, for me, more difficult to identify, but if you have a flair for watching races carefully or for judging a horse's condition in the parade ring, then these skills can pay handsome dividends. The aim of this book is to reveal which of the big handicaps regularly fall to 'dark' / 'form' / 'possible' / 'shock' horses. The usual reason for a race to fall regularly to a particular type of runner, is the position of the race in relation to other races. For example, the Royal Hunt Cup at Royal Ascot usually produces a 'shock' result because it is preceded by very few handicaps over the same distance run at the top class courses. The 8f and 12f handicaps at Royal Ascot for three year olds also regularly fall to 'dark' horses because they offer a tempting opportunity for horses lightly raced in the previous season.

How many races fall into the categories identified above? The result is rather surprising. The outcome of 52 named handicaps analysed in this book are:

20 'shock' results
26 'form' types
03 'dark' horses
03 'possible' horses

(If you want to see which races fall into which categories, see the Appendix QUICK REFERENCE: WINNING TYPES).

By 'shock' results, I mean that these are 'trappy' races, i.e. year in, year out, the results cannot be predicted on the basis of previous form. If the only advice you take from this book is to avoid these trappy races you will cut out a string of losers.

Given that many backers think that horses are always being 'laid out' for the big handicaps, it is surprising to see that only six (12%) fall into the 'dark' / 'possible' categories. More positively, it is surprising, given the generally low reputation of big handicaps, that just over half do fall into the 'form' category. In this category I have lumped together 3 kinds of races: races which are almost always won by horses following a form pattern; by horses which fit a statistical trend (or a combination of the two); and what I call 'neutral' races, those which are sometimes (i.e. in about four occasions out of ten) are won by a form/statistics runner. Incidentally, a quick check of Andrew Ayres's book, Trendsetters Review for the Flat (A statistical guide to 110 major races) (Raceform 2000) suggests that form horses win a lower proportion of the valuable non-handicap races. A similar check of the non-handicaps in the National Hunt season covered by Craig Thake's Ten Year Trends in Racing Post gives the same result – rather surprising, since the conventional wisdom is that form works out better in non-handicaps than in handicaps. It seems that precisely opposite is the case.

It is very important not to confuse any of these three types ('dark' / 'form' / 'possible') with what happens in the betting market. Anyone who follows racing closely for a few weeks will soon identify favourites or second favourites which do not fall into any of these categories. Conversely, a long-priced runner may in fact have a very strong chance as a 'form' horse. For example, although I did not make him a selection, THE EXTRA MAN (see chapter 6, 03 February 2001) had a fair chance on form and on the statistical record for the race. This chance was not reflected in the SP of 16-1, and anyone seeing the betting without knowing about the form would simply write this off as yet another unpredictable result typical of big handicaps. This combination of form horse/long price is quite unexpected, perhaps the most surprising feature of racing. In chapter 5 I explain how it arises.

A key point to note is that to bet successfully in big handicaps you must only follow the leading trainers. In chapters 3 and 4 I will identify the trainers who can be relied on to win big handicaps with 'form' horses. How did these trainers gain the enviable status of inclusion in my list? Analysing big handicaps, I have identified horses which should win on the basis of their form. Once a trainer has won at least two big handicaps with form horses, s/he has proved herself/himself him fit for inclusion in my list of leading trainers. Even the leading trainers do go in and out of form. But even here there are two advantages in focussing on the top stables. First, it is much easier to judge how well/badly a big stable is performing. If a small stable has two winners out of eight in the last 14 racing days (the figures are given in the Racing Post), the sample is too small, whereas if Mr/Ms. Big has the same strike rate, but ten winners out of 40, then that is much more significant. Secondly, the fortunes of the leading stables are of interest to the press, so if Mr/Ms. Big trainer X is having a quiet season, the reason will usually be reported.

Once a trainer has shown the ability to prepare horses for the big handicaps, s/he does not lose it - at least, I cannot remember any instances over the last two decades. What does happen is that trainers no longer have suitable candidates for the big handicaps. It is a change of fortune rather than a decline in ability which is the cause. Usually the circumstances are entirely beyond the trainer's control: an owner leaves along with most of the horses, a blood line becomes infertile. A good example is Guy Harwood. In the 1980s he was an absolute star trainer of big handicap winners, but in the 1990s, he found it much more difficult to find the right type of horse.

For our purposes, there is one major difference between Flat and NH trainers. Nearly all the big prizes on the Flat are won by the leading trainers. In fact, compared to only a generation ago, this tendency has increased dramatically. The cause is almost certainly the great concentration of ownership. By comparison, the trainer with a small string has a sporting chance in National Hunt racing, even at the Cheltenham Festival, which probably reflects the more dispersed ownership.

★★★

A Golden Age

Big handicaps have always proved profitable to follow, but this is a true Golden Age for backers who focus on this type of race. First of all, the sources of information are far more plentiful than ever before. Sadly for those with a romantic turn of mind, 'information' is not supplied by disreputable characters speaking in conspiratorial whispers from the side of their mouth in seedy public houses. In my system you can do perfectly well without insider information. However, if you do have reliable contacts inside a leading stable, the only questions you should ask are: is X fit enough for the forthcoming race? Has X recovered well from his previous race? The clichÈ, that this is 'The Information Age' applies as much to the turf, as it does to any area of life (apart from, of course, the British Government). Much more information than you will ever need is available for, sometimes literally, the price of a local phone call (the Internet) or a TV licence. Good websites are the Racing Post (www.racingpost.co.uk) and for Irish racing (www.irishfield.com). The databases on websites are particularly useful, as you can look up race results for up to a decade ago. In the past this would have meant access to a lot of rather bulky filing of back issues of newspapers for the current season, and shelves full of form books for past seasons. For the price of an ordinary TV licence (you don't really need satellite), you can watch all the big races live. The Morning Line is well worth watching on Saturday, as the cleverest men in racing share with you their ideas about the day's racing. Of these pay special attention to Jim McGrath, who works for the rather expensive Timeform organisation but gives you his views for free. And, as a bonus, the bookmaker Barry Dennis can always be relied on to identify likely false-priced favourites.

I regretted the demise of the Sporting Life, because I found its layout more attractive and readable than the paper which supplanted it, the Racing Post. It is perhaps ironic for a handicap enthusiast that it was the controversy over the running of a handicapper, TOP CEES, which seemed to hasten its end. But from a racing point of view the Racing Post (and its website, www.racingpost.co.uk) is a much better source of information.

If this is a Golden Age for backers, make the most of it, as the omens for the future of racing are not good. They are inauspicious for two reasons: the old-fashioned nature of the sport; and the shortcomings of racing's administrators. As a thrilling spectacle, when runners battle it out in the final furlong or several contenders jump the last together, racing can more than hold its own with any sport. And as sportsmen, jockeys still deserve the title, for genuinely sporting gestures are seen on the racecourse as nowhere else (except, perhaps, golf). But for the mass audience of today, stimulus-hungry and undiscriminating, football is not so much the 'beautiful game' as the 'simple game', possessing few finer points but offering many quick thrills. Of the traditional sports, racing is like cricket, complex and subtle and it can no longer compete for this audience.

In the last decade racing as a medium for gambling has become old-fashioned. During an afternoon's racing there is at most 20 minutes action in four hours, and few races last for more than four minutes. Most football matches offer at least 80 minutes hope to the backer, as the result is hardly ever clearcut until a few minutes before the final whistle. Other sports, such as cricket and golf, have an even longer betting time span. Nonetheless there is still a large enough public and sufficient betting interest to maintain racing as a commercially sound sport. Unfortunately, just as with cricket, racing's rulers are divided, lack a clear strategy, and do not know how to derive enough income from the bookmakers/broadcasting rights. In the last forty years their commercial ineptitude has missed two heaven-sent opportunities to create a sound financial basis for the sport: the licensing of betting shops in 1959; and the introduction of SIS transmission in the late 1980s. Let us hope that they don't miss the present opportunity, to derive an income from the Internet and satellite broadcasting. At beginning of the 21st century, racing, like cricket, is precariously clinging to its first rank status. Racing's rulers seem to have a classic small group mentality, unaware that their sport is not the centre of the universe. Like cricket, racing receives generous coverage in the daily papers quite disproportionate to the level of public interest. That a prominent official has been quoted as sayng that in the 21st century racing will overtake football as a leading sport shows what a dream world racing's administrators live in! If it fails to seize the present opportunity, in a decade's time racing could, along with cricket be in the second or third rank of popular sports. That said, in the short term, racing is in a fairly healthy state, so let us make the most of the opportunities. This book provides simple guidelines on how to do so, as follows:

Chapter 2 tells you how to weigh up any kind of handicap, big or small, All-Weather, Flat, or National Hunt.

Chapter 3 analyses the big Flat handicaps and identifies the leading trainers.

Chapter 4 does the same for National Hunt Racing.

Chapter 5 is a guide to betting on your selections.

Chapter 6 analyses a year at the races.

If you want to find a particular race quickly, there are two quick reference sections at the back of the book: ALPHABETICAL ORDER, BY COURSE WINNING TYPES.

Chapter 2: How to weigh up a handicap

The initial analysis of a big handicap is carried out in exactly the same way as any other handicap. If you are already familiar with this subject you can skip the next few paragraphs.

The theory of handicapping can be explained quite simply. In a handicap racehorses are allocated different weights so as to give every competitor a theoretically equal chance of winning. The weight carried by each horse is related to the handicap mark, determined by the official handicapper. Handicap marks are continually assessed in the light of recent performances. The re-assessment is based upon the following understanding of the relationship between weight and distance:

	up to 1/2 length	3/4 length	1 length
5f, 6f races	1 pound	2 pounds	3 pounds per length
7f, 8f races	1 pound	1 pound	2 pounds per length
9f+ races	no allowance	1 pound	1 pound per length
all National Hunt races	no allowance	no allowance	1 pound per length

However, handicapping is not an arithmetical exercise. If a horse wins a 12f Flat handicap easily by one length, and the handicapper considers that the victory was 'worth' four lengths, then he will increase the winner's mark by four pounds, not one. Having seen the race, you may disagree, and you may think that the winner was under- or over-rated by the handicapper. If a horse is rated, say, 95 by the official handicapper, and in my estimation he should be rated 96, then in my handicap book he is +1 (i.e. under-rated). If I think that the same horse should be rated 94, then he is –1 (i.e. over-rated).

A different problem arises in National Hunt racing. Look at the results of any half-dozen National Hunt handicaps, and you will immediately see the difficulty. Even at the major meetings, at least one-third of the races are won very easily by five lengths or more. In a few, the winning distances stretch to ten lengths or more, often with the winner being noticeably eased down before the line. How can such results be assessed by a handicapper? If the allowance of one pound per length was applied literally, winners would be raised, say, twelve pounds for a twelve length victory. If the principles set out above were followed, then it might seem logical to increase the mark of a horse which wins easily by twelve lengths, by fifteen pounds or more. Clearly such wins cannot be assessed in a literal way, and it is worth noting that the official handicapper does not attempt to do so. My solution is only to attempt to assess the of the closely contested races (wins of up to five lengths or so) and then weigh up the result in the usual way. Where a horse has won by more than this distance, I restrict the re-rating of the handicap mark to a range of 7-10 pounds. Because of this problem I find that my handicap assessments for National Hunt races vary much more from those for the Flat. As a result of this conservative approach, I sometimes find that my rating of a horse is -10 or more in relation to the official handicap.

Compiling your own private handicap is a fascinating exercise. If you would like to know how to do so in great detail, I recommend that you read How to Compile Your Own Handicap (Raceform 1997), by the then Raceform Private Handicapper, David Dickinson, and, for one sector of handicap racing, Sprint Handicaps Explained, by Jim Adams (Raceform 2000). However, it is extremely time-consuming, and, for the purpose of finding winners in big handicaps, not necessary. I only calculate my own handicap mark for the winners of the big handicap races, and I let the official handicapper worry about the also-rans and the minor handicaps. Not only does this save a great deal of time, it lets you focus on the essentials.

In compiling your handicap marks, you do exactly as the official handicapper does, except that you are only interested in handicapping the winner, whereas the official has to consider all the horses in the race. You watch the race, or read the reports in the Racing Post, and then make your own estimate of how much the winner's mark should be raised.

Strictly speaking, it is not necessary to watch any races at all, as the race-readers for Racing Post and Raceform are excellent, and you can generally rely on their judgements 105%. The only point in which I sometimes differ is their interpretation of how well a horse jumps, probably the most subjective aspect of race reading. If their reports suggest, or you notice, that a horse makes even the slightest mistake in jumping, then you should not attempt to give a handicap rating. For future reference, the horse should be discounted as an unreliable jumper, until he shows that his fencing is completely sound. This may seem like a very harsh judgement, but at the top level of competition, the less-than-reliable jumper is usually found out by his opponents. Even if such a horse does not fall when under pressure from his opponents, even one slight mistake can cause a fatal loss of momentum. Perhaps more important than calculating a mark for the winner is making a judgement about the form value of the race as a whole. If the race was run at a very slow early pace, or if the winner was left clear with a fence or two to go, then the value of the form is highly dubious. This type of judgement is the most difficult of all for amateur race-readers (among whom I most definitely class myself), as the tendency is to look at the leading group of runners throughout the race, whilst failing to take account of the overall pace. So if you are considering a particular horse as a selection, always go back to the report of the race, not just of the winner's performance (if you do not have access to the Internet I am afraid that this means keeping a bundle of clippings!). If the report suggests that this was for some reason a false result, then your selection should be immediately discounted.

In assessing the handicap mark, should you be influenced by the fact that a horse is from a leading stable? For instance, it is well-known that certain trainers are very skilled at placing late-developing three year olds to win handicaps by small margins so as to conceal from the handicapper the extent of their improvement. This is a perfectly legitimate, and well-known tactic. I suggest that you adopt exactly the same attitude as the official handicapper, i.e. you calculate the mark as if you did not know the identity of the trainer. As far as I can see, the authorities are even-handed between all trainers, and handicapping is no exception. The handicapper may well suspect that a horse is running in a certain way so as to gain a favourable mark, but they can, and do, only assess the record of public form and comply with the rules of racing. My view is that I wish we had officials of such integrity in other areas of public life. In fact, when trainers complain that their horses have been harshly treated by the official handicapper, they are almost always proven to be mistaken. There are two grounds for compiling: the re-rating of winners, and of losers. If a horse wins an 8f handicap in good style by four lengths, it does seem harsh to increase its mark by, say, 12 pounds. But in my experience, the squeals of protest from the horse's trainer are silenced by future victories. Some trainers do protest quite frequently, and the regular reader of the racing press will soon identify them. It is as pointless as arguing with the referee. More common than good winners being unfairly treated because of convincing wins, the opposite is often the case. The handicapper is very reluctant to reduce the mark of a horse which, after winning a race or two, then finds himself out of depth and unable to win. He needs to be released into lower grade company if he is to succeed: in racing terms, the horse is 'held off this mark'. But the handicapper cannot do this too quickly, as this would be unfair on the other horses. If a horse wins off a mark around 80, but is always beaten off 85, then it is reasonable for the handicapper to wait for the evidence from three or four races at the 85 level, before he begins to consider reducing the mark. Now there are trainers who quite legitimately try to supply the 'evidence' that the horse cannot win off 85, for example, running it over the 'wrong' course and distance. The handicapper is quite alert to these manoeuvres and makes his judgement accordingly. In any case, it is rare for this type of horse to win a big handicap. Whenever I read the phrase 'now back to a favourable mark and can return to winning ways' in the summing up of a big handicap, I am very sceptical. This is a ploy which frequently works well in the minor handicaps and at the lesser tracks, but is very hard to bring off in the big races.

The handicapper is continually assessing not only horses but races (as a guide to form). For example, when the handicapper assesses a race for the first time, a placed horse may be raised two or three pounds for running well though not winning. Two or three weeks later, in the light of the subsequent form of the other horses, the handicapper may come to the conclusion that the mark of the placed horse should be raised still further even though it has not run since. Again, this may seem to be rather unfair, but as a rule the handicapper is right to do so.

With all these points in mind, you should make your own assessment of a handicap rating. Remember that to be well in with the official handicap is not the key. In fact, I rarely find that my rating shows a plus mark in relation to the official handicap. As far as I am concerned, this does not matter, since my handicap marks serve only to rank horses relative to each other, and not to the official handicap.

And in my view, agonising over handicap marks is not one of the essentials. I would go further, and suggest that the official theory of handicapping is based on a misconception, that there is a calculable relationship between weight and distance, or that winners are stopped from winning their next race by the burden of extra weight.

What is the evidence that weight is the crucial factor? First, it has to be said that there are only two other options: the staggered start as in greyhound handicaps; and to borrow from cycle racing the idea of the 'time trial' i.e. the horse runs solo against the clock. Both are impractical for horse racing; and the latter would be a very dull spectacle indeed. The most plausible argument in favour of weight as the key to handicap races is the fact that non-handicap winners generally fail when running in a handicap. But is their failure caused by the equalising factor of weight? There is another explanation - speed. The ordinary non-handicap is usually run at a rather sedate pace, whereas handicaps tend to be much more competitive, so that the non-handicap winner is not so much burdened by weight, as unable to keep up the pace. It occurs to me that the weight theory may be self-perpetuating. The lightweights are sent off and make the pace because it is believed that weight tells...

The arguments against are the following.

Penalised horses. When horses run again before the official handicapper has had the opportunity to make a re-assessment, they carry a fixed penalty, and the more valuable the race, the higher the penalty. If weight were a disabling burden, you would expect the low-penalty (say, three pounds) horses to do better than those incurring a high penalty (say, seven pounds). The opposite is the case, which suggests that winning a higher class race is a far more important factor than excess weight.

Weight for age. Three year olds are given a concessionary weight allowance which is supposed to compensate for their physical weakness compared to their elders. Yet three year olds rarely beat older horses until the end of July, which suggests either that the weight allowance is not sufficient, or that no allowance could sufficiently compensate for their physical immaturity. I must say that I incline to the latter argument.

Reversing the form. Horse A beats horse B by one length in a 7f race. The handicapper is quite impressed by Horse A, and increases his rating by six pounds. They meet again, under similar conditions (a 7f race over the same course, distance and going), with the only difference being weight. Every commentator will say: 'meeting on revised terms, B's six pounds pull in the weights will enable him to beat A this time.' But 'reversing the form', a win for B under such circumstances, is very much the exception, not the rule.

Speed, not weight, is the key. The evidence for this argument is derived from All-Weather racing, where the relevance of speed figures is unquestionable. Horse A and horse B win two different races (but over the same course, distance and going) in a comparable style. When they meet, over the same course, distance and going, you (and other handicappers) may rate Horse A as being -2 in relation to the official ratings, and horse B at -5. Yet if horse B has recorded a faster time in the previous race than horse A, he will inevitably beat horse A.

A favourite phrase with journalists is 'anchored by the weight', i.e. as the horse rises in the handicap he reaches a point where this phrase seems to be apposite. But if I do not agree that he is being stopped by weight, what do I think is happening? I suggest that an improving horse finds himself in better and better class company, so that instead of finding one or two rivals of equal ability, he is constantly being challenged by five or six such rivals. The horse gets to a point in the handicap where he is not fast enough throughout the race to win again, so that when later on I write that a horse 'is held off this mark', I refer to speed rather than weight.

In my view there is only one type of race in which weight does seem to make an important difference. In handicap chases run over 3 miles and further, especially in soft going, weight can anchor the runners at the high end of the handicap. At this point, you could draw two conclusions. Either that the handicap system does not work, so perhaps handicaps should be avoided. Or agree with me, that handicap marks only serve to indicate the relative merits of different horses, and that perhaps other factors are more important in establishing reliable form. Finally, if ratings rather than weights are the key to understanding handicap form, it means that in analysing trends it is only necessary to check the pattern of ratings (and not weight) over a number of years. As stated above, the only exception is distance (3m+) handicap chases.

To continue with the form analysis. Once you have identified the form horses, and given them a rating, the following factors have to be checked. It seems like a long list, but with practice, as you will see in chapter 6, it does not usually take long to tick off each item.

Age
Class
Course
Distance
The Draw
Going
Recent Form
Sex
Speed
AGE

Three year olds rarely beat older horses until the Goodwood meeting at the end of July, and before this date can be discounted. On the Flat aged horses (7 years and older) do win the big handicaps over 2m+ (such as the Chester Cup, the Northumberland Plate and the Cesarewitch). However, few of these winners are from the leading stables, which generally do not retain aged horses on their racing strength. The only exception is I A Balding, who does occasionally win big handicaps with horses from this age group.

At sprint and middle distances, up to 2m, it is very rare for aged horses from any stable to win a big handicap, and they can be confidently discounted. The leading stables rarely keep on 6 year olds for this type of race, so when they do, look closely at their chances. In particular, John Dunlop has a good record with the few 6 year old handicappers he keeps in training.

A similar pattern can be detected in National Hunt racing. Horses older than ten are generally too old for the big handicaps, as, however well they continue to jump, they have begun to lose the turn of foot. They need an extended distance (more than 3m 4f) to bring their stamina into play. Likewise, 9 year old chasers and hurdlers have lost the turn of foot needed to win a 2m race, but can still win over 2m 4f+. Unlike their counterparts on the Flat, the leading National Hunt stables do retain a significant number of older horses, but they must have a live form chance to qualify for a selection.

CLASS

In racing, class tells. The big handicaps are like an exclusive club: to join, your credentials must be first class. Winners from second class courses need not apply for membership. The first class courses are:

FLAT
Ascot
Doncaster
Newbury
Newmarket
Sandown
The Curragh
York
NATIONAL HUNT
Aintree (National meeting)
Ascot
Cheltenham
Kempton
Newbury
Sandown

As you will have noted, these class distinctions do not apply rigidly in National Hunt racing in Ireland, for which it is not possible to lay down such hard-and-fast rules.

COURSE

How important is it to have won over the same course? For two courses, Newmarket and The Curragh, only course and distance winners should ever be considered.

For other courses, you need to make a rough-and-ready distinction between the two basic types: the flat and the uphill. The details are given in chapters 3 and 4, but are readily obtainable from the Racing Post. In general, it is usually unwise to follow form shown on a flat course if the next race is on an uphill finish. For example, if you are going to bet at Cheltenham (a searching uphill course), it is safest to rely on form shown at, say, Ascot or Sandown, which have a similar conformation.

The direction of a course, i.e. whether left- or right-handed is probably more important in NH racing, since some runners tend to jump consistently to one side. A horse which naturally jumps to the left will be unsuited by a course turning to the right.

DISTANCE

In the big Flat handicaps, if you follow a 'form' approach, it is a very sound rule only to back a horse over the distance at which it has already won. Distance winners are always over-represented in the winning statistics, i.e. on average they make up about 25% of the runners, but win 35% of the races. If you look at 'possible' winners, you might consider winners over a slightly shorter distance (but never more than the difference of a furlong). For example, winners of the 7f Victoria Cup at Ascot have sometimes won the Royal Hunt Cup at the Royal Ascot meeting.

But, with the exception of one race (the Cambridgeshire), you should always rule out a horse put back in distance. It always seems plausible to suggest that a winner over a flat 6f course could also win over a stiff uphill 5f. This is one of the big fallacies of racing, as horses hardly ever make this transition successfully. There are only two exceptions to these rules, the Ebor (York, August) and the Cambridgeshire (Newmarket, October). Winners over a shorter distance can win the Ebor, and the latter race is the only big handicap in which you should consider a winner over a longer distance.

I find that distance is the most difficult aspect of National Hunt racing, and it poses two problems. First, there are not the same standard set of distances as on the Flat. Give or take literally a few yards, 95% of Flat races fall into a set of similar distances. The equivalent in National Hunt racing would be if the distances were to increase in 2f steps from 2m to 4m, but they don't. So there are races at $2m^1/2f$, 2m 5f, 3m 1f and so on, distributed quite randomly throughout the season. Secondly, the records show that National Hunt winners are frequently capable of winning again over a shorter distance than their previous race. As we have seen, this happens very rarely in Flat racing.

Therefore, in National Hunt racing you will find very few horses with form at exactly the same distance. Horses which have been put back a short distance (say half a furlong, i.e. 110 yards) can win, and should not be excluded on the grounds of distance. But if the distance is a furlong or further, runners being put back in distance should always be excluded.

However, it is not necessary to be so restrictive about runners over a longer distance, say up to four furlongs further. The form book shows that National Hunt horses are not so tied to particular distances, and can win again over significantly longer distances (but not over more than four furlongs).

In addition to this significant difference between the two codes, there are national differences. National Hunt horses in Britain seem to be less specialised in distance than on the Flat, whereas in Ireland, horses under both codes run over a much greater variety of distances. Such specialisation is a relatively recent phenomenon. Until the beginning of the 20th century, it was quite common for runners to aim at (and occasionally win) the Autumn Double, of the Cambridgeshire (9f) and the Cesarewitch (2m 2f), a feat which would be unthinkable today. Does form work out best at particular distances? On the Flat there is a slight advantage at 7f and 12f. Seven furlong races require a particular combination of speed and stamina, less evident in 6f or 8f races. Over the classic distance of 12f, distance specialists have a very good record. Both distances catch out the non-staying speedsters, and the non-speedy stayers. Handicap chases and hurdles at around 3m are a good test of the speed-stamina combination. Any doubts about stamina or jumping ability will be revealed without fail, but to be a clean-jumping plodder is not enough, as some pace is required. Handicap hurdles over this distance can be won by runners with uncertain stamina, but not handicap chases.

THE DRAW

Graham Wheldon's thoroughly researched book, Backing the Draw for Profit (Raceform 2000) tells you as much as, possibly more than, you would ever want to know about the effects of the draw. It shows that there is a persistent and predictable draw bias in only two cases: races at Beverley over 5f and 7f 100 yards when the going is good or faster; and over 5f and 6f at Hamilton, when the going is good to soft or softer. Although his findings are based on only two seasons, I have found that they are valid over a much longer period. However, these results are of no use to the big handicap specialist. The only big handicap in which the draw bias seems established in advance is not mentioned in Wheldon's book: in the Ebor winners are usually drawn 1-10.

A draw bias which cannot be reliably anticipated does seem to affect three big handicaps, all over 6f: the Wokingham (Royal Ascot), the Stewards' Cup (Goodwood) and the Ayr Gold Cup. In most years, the going is much better on one side of the course, and the field usually divides into two parts as one group of runners splits off to seek the better ground.

Every year there is much agonising before these races about the possible effect of the draw. It is pointless to pay attention to these speculations. A much more promising idea is to look at the 'outliers', i.e. in a race which is dominated by horses drawn on a certain part of the course, those horses which ran well without winning to finish close up from an unfavourable draw.

The Wokingham does not divide in this way very often, but it can occasionally provide a useful pointer. In 1992, the first six home were drawn 29,

28, 21, 17, 24, 23, so the runner drawn 17 (LOCHSONG) had run much better than her placing suggested. LOCHSONG went on to win the Stewards' Cup.

The Stewards' Cup is the most fruitful source for 'outliers'. In 1996, the 'outlier' was WILDWOOD FLOWER drawn 7, as the first five home were drawn 29, 23, 28, 15, 7. WILDWOOD FLOWER won a good handicap at Goodwood later that season, and the Ayr Gold Cup in the next season. In 1998, in a 29 runner field, the first four home were drawn 28, 25, 29, 23, then HARMONIC WAY (18), NIGHT SHOT (11), MASHA-IL (16). HARMONIC WAY won the Stewards' Cup in 1999 and the Wokingham in 2000; NIGHT SHOT won next time at York, when put back to a suitable distance, at 4-1; and MASHA-IL won quite a valuable handicap over the course and distance, next time out, at 6-1.

The field for the Ayr Gold Cup usually divides more distinctly and more frequently than the other two, but at this late stage in the season, there are hardly any opportunities left for sprint handicappers.

GOING

Changes in going are the most frequent factor in causing 'shock' results. Generally, there is no point in guessing whether a possible selection will act on going over which he has not won previously. It makes more sense to restrict your selections to those which have shown that they can act on today's going. Not all of the leading trainers are very good at assessing how well a runner will handle going he has not previously encountered. There are only a few exceptions. The exceptions are: Cumani, Dunlop, and Gosden on the Flat; and, for National Hunt racing, Pipe and Twiston-Davies. So if a change of going is forecast, always read the press carefully on the day of the race. Some trainers will clearly state their views about how well their runners will cope with certain types of going. This invaluable information is often ignored by punters, to the extent of making a runner favourite, despite the trainer's explicit statement that it will be unsuited by the going. There is another way of answering the question, whether a selection will act on going over which he is untested. If you are skilled at 'reading' a horse's action, watch the runners going down to post. When the going is soft, you should look for a 'round' action and rule out the horses with a 'high' or 'sharp' action; and a horse with a 'round' or 'low' action is unlikely to act on good to firm going. Unfortunately, these are difficult skills to acquire, unless you have had some experience of working with horses.

If the weather is changeable you must always leave your selection until the last moment, so as to check the state of the going. Even the going reports issued by the courses on the race are often rather vague. It would be of great help to all involved if the BHB were to adopt the French system of assessing the state of the turf using a 'penetrometer', an instrument like the common garden tool the dibber, about 30 cms long and made of metal, which is used for measuring moisture.

At one or two courses even a few showers can cause the going to change rapidly and unevenly, whereas at others it requires a steady downpour to cause significant changes in the going. Compare, for example, Doncaster and York, in the same part of the country. The going can get quite heavy at Doncaster, particularly in October and November, but it takes a steady soaking. More importantly, the course seems to become evenly wet, so that the results are not unpredictable as the races are won by confirmed heavy going specialists. At York, far less rain causes far more 'shock' results, as the course seems to get wet in patches, giving false going so that even the confirmed soft going specialists do not give their best performance. A careful study of going preferences as revealed by the form book and trainers' interviews can keep you on your guard, so that 'shock' results are not a surprise. In the case of longer term patterns, such as a wet Flat season or a dry National Hunt season, you simply have to accept that you will probably make fewer selections. In Flat racing, if the going is consistently soft, and not changeable, the good ground horses, by far the majority in any stable, have to stay at home. The reverse is true for National Hunt. The going patterns over a season are the most significant factor determining the number of selections you will make.

HANDICAP FORM

With the exception of only two races (the Britannia, Royal Ascot; the Ebor, York August), there is one golden rule about handicap form: Never follow non-handicap form into a handicap

A runner must have won some sort of handicap in order to be considered as a potential winner of a big handicap. In National Hunt there is the further qualification, that to be considered for a handicap chase, a runner must have previously won a handicap chase, and not just a handicap hurdle.

It might seem that this rule would allow you to rule out of consideration very few horses in big handicaps, but sometimes up to a third of the runners fail this test.

RECENT FORM

How recent is 'recent'?

I eliminate runners which have not won a handicap in the current season. In Flat racing, it is obvious what this means, but since the National Hunt season now runs without a break, where do we draw the line? I suggest that, for big handicaps, the National Hunt season in Britain begins in mid-October and ends on the last Saturday of April.

Unless the circumstances are quite exceptional, I also eliminate runners which have not won in their last two starts, even if that victory happened quite recently. I look very closely at horses which have won their penultimate race and then been unsuccessful. If the latter race was over an unsuitable course, distance or going, I retain the horse as a possible selection, the final decision to be made on other grounds.

Even the most gifted trainers find it very difficult to keep a horse at race fitness without visiting the racecourse, so I discount horses which have not run for more than 90 days. Every season, we do see trainers perform this most difficult of feats, but unless you are able to judge the condition of a horse in the parade ring, it is best to refrain from betting. In National Hunt racing, I immediately eliminate any runner which fell, was pulled up, unseated his rider, and, perhaps rather drastically and unfairly, was brought down, last time out. I would prefer to wait to see if the horse has recovered his ability and his confidence in the present race, rather than taking a chance that he has not done so.

SEX

No big handicaps are restricted to horses of one sex, and, for once in life, sex does not generally have to be taken into account. However, the following points should be noted. Fillies and mares can show spectacularly improved form in a very short time, particularly in the latter part of the Flat season (from August onwards). As the days get shorter, they stop coming into season, and their performance often shows a striking improvement. Mares seem to be subject to these dramatic changes throughout the National Hunt season.

As a group, fillies and mares show a marked preference for certain long distances (12f+ on the Flat, 3m+ in National Hunt) and can compete on equal terms with colts and geldings over these distances. Their natural extra stamina (common to females of nearly all species) comes into play so that the further they go, the better they run. This is because fillies and mares metabolise more fat than their male or neutral competitors, so that at the longer distances, when runners switch from anaerobic to aerobic (from burning glycogen to fat/carbohydrate), they have more fuel left to burn.

Fillies and mares also seem to act very well on soft and heavy going, perhaps because of their light build. As individuals, if they show a preferences for this type of going, it tends to be much more marked than that of colts and geldings, so that they may simply fail to act at all on good/firm going.

Two final words of caution. More than any other type of horse, fillies and mares can be subject to temperament and put in an unexplainably poor performance. Ideally, their behaviour should be watched very closely, right up to the point of entering the stalls. You are looking for any signs of nervousness and not being in the right mood (e.g. sweating heavily, being over-active, 'skittering' on the way to the start). Three year olds seem to be most subject to these hormonally-induced changes, as older fillies and mares are much calmer. In big handicaps, it does not matter at all whether a horse is a colt or a gelding, when you are considering its chances. Geldings are tough, reliable and consistent, and these qualities come to the fore in National Hunt racing, where most of the runners are geldings. Their ability to endure a punishing race is ideal for the severe test of carrying weight over obstacles. Much more so than in Flat racing, a gelding which has had to be ridden quite hard in the closing stages can win again given sufficient time to recuperate.

SPEED

Speed figures are not of much use in Flat racing, let alone in National Hunt. Occasionally, although less so than a decade ago, the position of the starting stalls is moved (because of changes in the going) so that the distance of the race is changed, and therefore the speed is inaccurately calculated. More seriously, long and careful study has convinced me that it is difficult when looking at speed figures to make an appropriate allowance for different types of going. I have compiled a record of the winning times of the major sprint handicaps run over the last two decades, but it is only of limited use. In their next two handicaps, most of these winners could not be considered as selections, so it was statistically impossible to draw any conclusions.

All-Weather racing is not subject to these objections (changes in going, and in race distance), but it does fall prey to a third. Two races may be run in the same overall time, but at a different rhythm. In Race A, the early pace is sedate, the final sprint furious; in Race B, there is a strong gallop throughout. The difference could only be identified objectively if sectional times, recording, say the time at the end of the first and fourth furlongs, were available. James Willoughby (Topspeed in Racing Post) has made a good attempt to provide these times for some races, but the only reliable solution would be by electrical timing at key distances, such as is available for U.S. racing and greyhound racing. Sectional timing is not available at any British or Irish race-course, and it is such a low spectator priority that it is unlikely to be provided.

Before I leave the general subject of weighing up handicaps, I would like to mention two intriguing questions to which I do not have a definite answer.

Some handicaps, particularly National Hunt races, are very 'unbalanced', i.e. there is an uneven distribution of weight throughout the handicap. Consider the following typical example, the Ladbroke Handicap, run at Cheltenham on 14 March 2000 (this race is also analysed in chapter 4). In a 24 runner field, the top weight, 12 st 0lbs, was carried by only one runner, while there were several horses on the bottom weight, 10 st 0lbs. If the weights had been evenly distributed, the mid-point weight would occur at 11st 0lbs, with 12 runners above and 12 below. In fact, only four runners carried 11st 0lbs and above, with the remaining 20 all below. This explains what an 'unbalanced' handicap is, but it does not answer the question, is it safer to bet in 'balanced' or 'unbalanced' handicaps? I have not come up with any firm conclusions to date.

The second question is related to longer-term trends. A rough indication of the competitiveness of a race is given by the mark carried by the top weight. If this mark is low compared to previous runnings of the race, it suggests that this is a weak renewal of the contest. The question is, does form work out better in competitive or uncompetitive renewals? I suspect that more reliable results occur in more competitive races, but I do not have enough data to give a definite answer.

ANALYSIS OF A HANDICAP

My methods may seem rather complicated, but in practice the system is perfectly straightforward. In fact, looking for 'form' horses in this way is a valuable simplification. If you consider 'possible' horses (a horse running in an 8f race which has only won at 7 furlongs), then you will probably have to evaluate all the runners in a race. I simply ignore these 'possibilities', except in certain races which are often won by this type of horse, so be on your guard. These races are identified in Chapters 3 and 4.

To show how the system works, I have analysed four types of races, all taken from recent seasons (1995-2000): * an averagely complicated National Hunt race;

* a Flat handicap which looks very daunting, but took just a few minutes to weigh up;

* a Flat handicap which required a knowledge of form trends for the particular race;

* a more than averagely complicated Flat handicap.

In two cases you will see that even after the most careful analysis, you will not be able to make a selection. The first example is an averagely complicated National Hunt race.

15 March 2000 CHELTENHAM
Mildmay of Flete Challenge Cup 2m 4^{1}/2f handicap chase
Going: Good to Firm
The race looks daunting, a 20 runner handicap with lots of good-looking form.

6F12	UPGRADE	6-11-10	M C Pipe
3-7U1	MAKOUNJI*	6-11-7	N J Henderson
1112	NATIVE CHARM	8-11-0	C P Morlock
32P1	INN AT THE TOP	8-10-8	J RTurner
4534	NORTHERN STARLIGHT	9-10-7	M C Pipe
1F19	SIR DANTE	9-10-7	R Rowe
1323	STORM DAMAGE	8-10-6	P F Nicholls
3-F27	DAWN LEADER	9-10-6	E Stanners
21R2	GO ROGER GO	8-10-5	E J O'Grady
24P1	DARK STRANGER	9-10-3	M C Pipe
7-133	FEATHERED LEADER	8-10-0	A L T Moore
24-41	KING OF SPARTA	7-10-0	J G Portman
1122	NOSAM	10-10-0	N B Mason
1U33	NICHOLLS CROSS	8-10-0 E	J O'Grady
6214	SKYCAB	8-10-0	J T Gifford
4534	CLASSY LAD	10-10-0	A Thornton
P6PP	JACK DOYLE	9-10-0	N A Twiston-Davies
1341	THE BREWMASTER	8-10-0	Ian Williams
2125	NEW INN	9-10-0	S Gollings
3523	GLAMANGLITZ	10-10-0	P T Dalton

* the dash in the form line, 3-7U1, indicates a seasonal break

You can take two short-cuts in analysing a race: focus only on the leading trainers; or check the statistical trend, to see if it makes a significant reduction in the number of runners to be checked. However, as we shall see in chapter 3, it is important to have a record of the trends not only in terms of the statistics, but also of the form. Unless we check all the runners, we will not know whether there are any form patterns to the race.

Taking trouble will pay off in the long run, so let's be systematic. Remember that the basic categories for analysis are:

AGE
CLASS
COURSE
DISTANCE
DRAW, THE
GOING
HANDICAP FORM
RECENT FORM
SEX
SPEED

In National Hunt racing, you can forget about the DRAW, SEX (for once!) and SPEED. Two of the categories can be applied immediately, without even looking at the form: AGE and RECENT FORM.

On the grounds of AGE, you can eliminate:

NOSAM	**10 year old**
CLASSY LAD	**10 year old**
GLAMANGLITZ	**10 year old**

Only three, but it is a start.

Eliminating runners on the grounds of RECENT FORM, i.e. either have not won this season or in their most recent two races, is more productive, as you cut out:

NORTHERN STARLIGHT	**4534**
STORM DAMAGE	**1323**
DAWN LEADER	**3-F27**
GO ROGER GO	**21R2**
FEATHERED LEADER	**7-133**
NICHOLLS CROSS	**1U33**
JACK DOYLE	**P6PP**
NEW INN	**2125**

Another eight eliminated, leaving nine possibles. Now we have to start to look at the small print of the form. Handicap form is the first category to check. You can immediately eliminate the two runners which have not won a handicap chase:

UPGRADE
SKYCAB

The next category is DISTANCE, i.e. runners which have won either over the distance of the race, or (in National Hunt racing only) within 4 furlongs shorter. In this race, that means winning between $2^{1}/2$m and 2m 5f. All the horses not so far eliminated have won over this distance.

Now, after about ten minutes checking, the field has been reduced to seven runners, with the grounds for elimination given in the right hand column.

UPGRADE	**Not won a handicap chase**
MAKOUNJI	

NATIVE CHARM	
INN AT THE TOP	
NORTHERN STARLIGHT	Recent form
SIR DANTE	
STORM DAMAGE	Recent form
DAWN LEADER	Recent form
GO ROGER GO	Recent form
DARK STRANGER	
FEATHERED LEADER	Recent form
KING OF SPARTA	
NOSAM	Age
NICHOLLS CROSS	Distance
SKYCAB	Not won a handicap chase
CLASSY LAD	Age
JACK DOYLE	Recent Form
THE BREWMASTER	
NEW INN	Recent form
GLAMANGLITZ	Age

We have now arrived at a shortlist of eight:

MAKOUNJI
NATIVE CHARM
INN AT THE TOP
SIR DANTE
STORM DAMAGE
DARK STRANGER
KING OF SPARTA
THE BREWMASTER

This is the most pernickety stage. Firstly, check the GOING performances. All 7 have proven form over the going, so none can be eliminated on those grounds. Secondly, before looking at their handicap marks, we look carefully at their jumping record. MAKOUNJI made a mistake last time out, and is immediately eliminated.

Finally, look more closely at their handicap marks. NATIVE CHARM and SIR DANTE are running off the same or higher marks respectively as when they were beaten last time out with no extenuating circumstances. Therefore they are both held off their current mark, giving them no chance at this competitive meeting.

So now we have to assess handicap performance carefully. here is the course and distance record, together with my assessment of the handicap marks in relation to the official rating:

+2 INN AT THE TOP	**Doncaster 2m 3f**
-3 SIR DANTE	**Kempton 2m 4f**
-3 KING OF SPARTA	**Wincanton 2m 5f**
-4 DARK STRANGER	**Leicester 2m 4f**
-15 THE BREWMASTER	**Newbury 2m 2$\frac{1}{2}$f**

Now look at the COURSE suitability of each runner's form. On this criterion, INN AT THE TOP, SIR DANTE, and THE BREWMASTER, can be eliminated, because of winning at a flat track, whereas Cheltenham has a severe uphill finish. This leaves only KING OF SPARTA and DARK STRANGER, both reasonably in at -3 and -4. The final test is CLASS. Wincanton is a galloping course, but not in the same class as Cheltenham, so KING OF SPARTA can be ruled out. DARK STRANGER has won at a first class course, Ascot, but his most recent win was at Leicester, which is not a good enough class for a competitor at the Cheltenham Festival. In the end, after about 20 minutes for analysing an averagely complicated race, there is no selection. This is always frustrating, but you have exercised your skills, and now move on to the next opportunity.

I have described the process exactly as carried out. It seems rather long-winded, but it is systematic, and with only a little practice, it becomes a matter of habit.

The result was:
1 DARK STRANGER
2 NATIVE CHARM
3 INN AT THE TOP
4 SIR DANTE

The second example looked more daunting, but was in fact much simpler.

28 October 1995 NEWMARKET Rowley Mile

Ladbroke Autumn 8f handicap

Going: good to firm

1000	KAYVEE	6-10-0	G Harwood
0211	NIGHT DANCE	3-9-7	G Lewis
0131	TARAWA	3-9-2	N A Callaghan
0310	WEAVER BIRD	5-9-2	H Candy
4134	SHARP REVIEW	7-9-2	J R Jenkins
3132	WESTERN FAME	3-9-1	J L Dunlop
0413	RON'S SECRET	3-9-1	J W Payne
100-0	ETHBAAT	4-9-1	W R Muir
6-104	DELTA SOLEIL	3-8-13	P W Harris
4000	BILLY BUSHWHACKER	4-8-13	Mrs Reveley
5501	STONE RIDGE	3-8-13	R Hannon
2600	WAKEEL	3-8-12	G Duffield
0131	COMMANCHE COMPANION	5-8-11	T J Naughton
3220	BALL GOWN	5-8-10	D T Thom
0064	ERTLON	5-8-10	C E Brittain
2235	COOL EDGE	4-8-9	M H Tompkins
1012	MO-ADDAB	5-8-9	A C Stewart
0000	OUR RITA	6-8-9	J D Scargill
4050	CELESTIAL CHOIR	5-8-9	J L Eyre
0020	SERIOUS	5-8-8	Lady Herries

0205	PAY HOMAGE	7-8-8	I A Balding
0025	COUNTRY LOVER	4-8-7	Lord Huntingdon
1212	CONSPICUOUS	5-8-7	L G Cottrell
5504	CLIFTON FOX	3-8-6	J A Glover
5301	SAMBA SHARPLY	4-8-5	A Hide
4102	CELTIC FRINGE	3-8-5	H R A Cecil
1050	MA PETITE ANGLAISE	3-8-4	W Jarvis
2100	APOLLONO	3-8-4	J R Fanshawe
1000	SAIFAN	6-8-4	D Morris

The line-up looks tricky. In their last 116 races, the 29 runners have notched up 22 wins. Surely, finding a winner in 29-runner field in a 'back-end' handicap at Newmarket is impossible? Most experts would advise you to bet on two drops of water running down a windowpane instead.

20 of the runners have won a handicap over the distance. In fact, once you remember that at Newmarket you should only consider course and distance winners, there are just three contestants.

SAIFAN has won here in the past, but was held by STONE RIDGE last time out
STONE RIDGE won 14 October 1995
TARAWA won 12 October 1995

All that remained was to estimate the handicap marks of STONE RIDGE and TARAWA. As it happened, I rated them equally at -3 in relation to the official handicap, setting me something of a puzzle. In this case, which does not arise very often, I usually find it the best policy to my bet and back both horses to win, especially since in a large field there will be some competitive prices. In the event, TARAWA won in commanding style, at 9-1, while STONE RIDGE (12-1), who won the Lincoln in 1996, found the pace too hot and finished ninth. The net profit of 4 points is the equivalent of backing a 4-1 winner, showing the soundness of the betting strategy. The next handicap is one which requires a knowledge of form trends for the particular race.

06 November 1999 DONCASTER November Handicap 12f

Going: Soft

5385	ABYAAN	4-9-10	J H M Gosden
2732	MURGHEM	4-9-4	R Hughes
9323	AKBAR	3-9-1	J Fanning
270/0	QUAKERS FIELD	6-9-0	G L Moore
0994	STAR PRECISION	5-8-12	G B Balding
2246	ROBIN LANE	4-8-12	M Johnson
7110	MONTECRISTO	6-8-12	R Guest
0308	RED RAMONA	4-8-12	J Akehurst
10-32	LORD LAMB	7-8-9	Mrs Reveley
4212	MINIVET	4-8-9	T D Easterby
3003	PUNISHMENT	8-8-7	K O Cunningham-Brown
6052	EVANDER	4-8-7	J Fortune

1390	ARABIAN MOON	3-8-3	C E Brittain
3330	CARLYS QUEST	5-8-0	J Neville
1162	FLOSSY	3-7-12	C W Thornton
3695	NORCROFT JOY	4-7-11	N A Callaghan
1369	MACCA LUNA	4-7-9	Miss S E Hall

The form trend is that the race favours horses with good form at Haydock and Newmarket within the last six weeks. There are 9 distance winners, but basing ourselves on this form trend, we only have to look closely at two: FLOSSY and MINIVET.

FLOSSY won at Haydock over 12f, and was then beaten over 10f and 13f. MINIVET also won a 12f race at Haydock, and was then beaten over $10^1/2$f at the same course. Our estimate of the handicap marks was:
- FLOSSY
- 6 MINIVET

As usual, sex confused the issue, so there was no selection. As FLOSSY had not won either of her last two races, her recent form was equivocal; and her stable has not won many top class handicaps. On the other hand, she was a progressive 3 y o filly running over the sort of ground which often suits fillies. You expect fillies to confound those like myself who interpret the form book strictly, and so she did. The final example in this chapter is more complicated than average.

14 August 1999 NEWMARKET July Course 7f handicap
Going: Good

24-52	MUBRIK	4-9-12	J H M Gosden
4020	HO LENG	4-9-11	Miss L A Perratt
8217	GRANGEVILLE	4-9-8	I A Balding
7-150	COOL EDGE	8-9-7	M H Tompkins
1800	ICE	3-8-13	M Johnston
2-921	CRUINN A BHORD	4-8-13	A C Stewart
4028	SALTY JACK	5-8-12	V Soane
4247	FAMILY MAN	6-8-11	J R Fanshawe
2-131	TAYIF	3-8-9	J W Payne
0090	TEMERAIRE	4-8-6	D J S Cosgrove
0060	CONSORT	6-8-6	Mrs A J Perrett
4141	TOPTON	5-8-1	P Howling
1132	TEOFILO	5-8-0	A J McNae
0348	JUST NICK	5-7-11	W R Muir
2303	BINTANG TIMOR	5-7-10	W J Musson
98-00	MASTER MAC	4-7-10	N Hamilton
5-040	BUONA SERA	3-7-10	W R Muir

Although there is a simple rule that only course and distance winners should be considered at Newmarket, this is an example of a race which is still quite complicated to analyse. There were 4 course and distance winners:

CRUINN A BHORD
HO LENG
GRANGEVILLE
TEOFILIO

In terms of RECENT FORM, HO LENG could be ruled out, as he had not won that season. None of the others could be eliminated because of AGE or GOING, and the DRAW is irrelevant. So the handicap marks have to be calculated carefully as they are the only basis for making the selection. In my estimation, they were:

+2 CRUINN A BHORD
-1 TAYIF
-1 GRANGEVILLE

The final step is usually to look at the record of the trainers involved, but as I explain in the next chapter, for this course and distance the identity of the trainer is irrelevant. So in our final example, there is a clear-cut selection, CRUINN A BHORD, a winner at 7-1.

Chapter 3: The big handicaps: Flat

The Flat season has a very pleasing rhythm. It begins rather slowly for the first 12 weeks, building up to Royal Ascot in mid June; moves steadily on for the next 11 weeks to the Doncaster St Leger meeting at the beginning of September; pauses for three weeks; and then dashes on to a climax with the final meetings at Newmarket and Doncaster. Form works out in a series of overlapping periods:

The build up to Royal Ascot. Note that several of the big handicaps at Royal Ascot mark the end, and not the beginning of the season, for the winners. The other big handicaps can be taken as preparation for the Goodwood meeting at the end of July.

The high season: from Royal Ascot to the Newmarket Houghton meeting.

The final period. From the Newmarket Houghton meeting at the end of September, recent form is vital

The more predictable big handicaps fall in the second 'half' of the season, from the July meeting at Goodwood onwards. The handicaps at Royal Ascot are the hinge point. Up to and including this meeting, most of the big handicaps fall into the 'dark / possible / trappy' categories. The first part of the old saying, don't start betting until the Royal Ascot meeting and finish with the Doncaster St Leger meeting, generally holds true. However, I do not agree with the second part, as the Newmarket and Doncaster meetings in the last six weeks of the season usually throw up some good bets. This chapter and the next one, on National Hunt racing, organise the big handicaps by course, so that on the day of racing you can easily find the information. The period over which handicaps are analysed runs from 1990-99.

ASCOT

A fine galloping right-handed course, 14f round, with an uphill finish. Although it is a testing course, Ascot form only seems to work out well at the Goodwood July meeting. This may be due to the character of the races rather than the course, as apart from the Royal Meeting (June) and the Festival meeting (September), the racing is often unexpectedly moderate.

The course can become very waterlogged rather quickly, so make sure that you have the latest information on the state of the going.

Victoria Cup 7f handicap
Age: not significant
Rating: no trend

One of the metropolitan handicaps which has entered into a decline. It used to be one of the early season big-betting races, but, in real terms, the prize money has fallen steadily so that the race is no longer an attraction to the leading stables.

This is a handicap for 'possible' rather than 'form' winners, i.e for a horse which has run well without winning this season. The irreplaceable R Ake-hurst won twice with such runners, SKY CLOUD (1991) and TREGARON (1997). The Victoria Cup is not a pointer to other handicaps over the same distance. However, in the 1990s, the only two horses (FACE NORTH 1994; YEAST 1996) to attempt the Victoria Cup - Royal Hunt Cup (8f) double were successful.

ROYAL ASCOT
Ascot Stakes 20f handicap
Age: not significant
Rating: the average rating (78) is rather low

This is not a 'form' race, since half of the last 10 winners in had not scored during the current season. It is also difficult to weigh up in terms of form over the distance.

Since this race is not preceded by any big handicaps over the same distance, it has rather an isolated position in the season. In fact, there are very few races in the entire calendar which are run over 2m 4f or longer. The only handi-caps before this race which approach this distance are the 2m 2f handicap run at the first meeting at Doncaster and the 2m 2f Chester Cup. These are useless for form purposes, as the Doncaster race is too early in the season, and Chester form is too unreliable. Martin Pipe often has a crack at this race, which he has won twice with BALASANI (1993) and SWEET GLOW (1994), out of six runners.

In terms of both form and statistics this is a trappy race which should be avoided.

The Ascot Stakes is followed by only one race, the Goodwood Cup, at the Goodwood July meeting, over the same distance. This would seem a rather obvious 'double' to aim at, but only three recent winners have attempted to do so:

1995 HARLESTONE BROOK L 15-8f
1996 SOUTHERN POWER W 4-1 FPF
1999 HIGH AND MIGHTY W 2-1f
Britannia 8f 3 y o handicap
Rating: no pattern

This is a race for 'dark' horses. Half the winners in the 1990s had not won a handicap, and all these winners were rated 84-94, which means that they had begun to move up the handicap scale. In the last 20 years, the winners of this race had won previously at minor tracks such as Beverley, Brighton, Carlisle, and Leicester.

There is one key trend. This race is hardly ever won by one of the smaller yards, and none did so in the 1990s. A careful study of the results shows that while the leading trainers do make a number of entries, there is usually a tell-tale clue to the ones they really fancy. The one exception is Henry Cecil. Although he has had only a few runners, his wins with PROTECTION (1985) and PYTHIOS (1999) were very difficult to forecast. The only factor which they had in common was that they had not won a handicap. It is best to look for winners last time out over the distance at either a good class or a testing course with an uphill finish. In this category there were two winners in the 1990s:

1993 SHOW FAITH (Hannon, Newmarket 8f stakes) W 6-1f
1995 MEDAILLE MILITAIRE (Dunlop, Newcastle 8f stakes) W 4-1f

ALJATHAAB seemed to have the right profile for Gosden in 1994, winning a 8f maiden race Ayr but was a loser here. Gosden has also had winners from unusual races with NORTH SONG (1996; won a 9f Goodwood maiden), and PLAN B (1998; still a maiden). At a slightly earlier date (1984), TOR-WAR scored for Cumani, after winning a stakes over the distance at Goodwood. He also scored with a 7f winner stakes winner at Brighton, DALLAS (1986).

This is not a particularly good handicap to win, as for many of the winners it represents the peak of the performance, and they cannot go higher, or even win further races. The last winner to do really well in subsequent races was DALLAS. In particular, winners of this race ran badly in the 8f handicaps at the Newmarket July meeting or at Goodwood. AJAAD scraped home in a measly 5 runner handicap at Newcastle (1991), but in doing so he was the most successful Britannia winner in the 1990s.

Duke of Edinburgh (formerly Bessborough) 12f handicap

Age: 6/10 winners 4 y o

The age trend is less impressive than it seems, as it is disproportionate to the number of 4 year old competitors.

Rating: 8/10 rated 87 and higher

This is one of the less unpredictable races at the meeting, since it is usually won by a fairly exposed horse, just as the rating pattern suggests. The winner has usually won a handicap over the distance, and last time out winners have a fairly good record. Unlike its 3 year old counterpart, the King George V, the prize usually goes to a horse which has won a handicap over this distance.

This is much more predictable than the other Royal Ascot handicaps, as four of the last five winners had previously won a handicap. Winners of handicaps over the distance last time out have a good record, as follows:

1993	BLACKPATCH HILL	-10*	Dunlop Doncaster	L 4-1f
1995	SON OF SHARP SHOT	-2	Dunlop Goodwood	W 5-1
1995	ZARALASKA	-4	Cumani York 2nd	100-30
1997	HOH EXPRESS	-4	Balding Goodwood	L 14-1
1999	BLUEPRINT	-4 S	toute Newmarket	W 4-1f

* refers to my handicap rating

The winners tend to be fairly reliable handicappers who can go on to win future races. In the last 10 years, the record in handicaps of subsequent winners of this race from leading stables is as follows:

1992	SPINNING	W 16-1 FPF*
1995	SON OF SHARP SHOT	L 11-4f
1997	ZARALASKA	W 5-1
1998	GREEK PALACE	L 2-1f

* FPF = false-priced favourite

BLUEPRINT did not run in another handicap.

King George V 12f 3 y o handicap

Rating: 10/10 rated 81+

The statistical trend seems clear enough, but in terms of form this is a race with a wildly varying pattern of winners. It is a handicapper's nightmare, as most winners had hardly any two year old form, and not much more at three years either. There are only two clear signs, neither of which enable you to eliminate many non-contenders. Maiden winners are very rare, the first for 25 years being ELMUTABAKI in 1999. All the winners have been from powerful stables, but these stables usually account for more runners (at least half a dozen) than in any other Royal Ascot handicap. Twelve furlongs is the Classic distance, and winners here are often well-bred disappointments who have not come to hand quickly enough to make the Derby grade.

Otherwise this is a game of two very puzzling halves.

4/10 winners had not previously won a handicap. Winners following this path were all rated 90 or less and carried no more than 8-12. The other six, the previous handicap winners, were all (bar MIDNIGHT LEGEND, 1994) exactly the opposite: they were rated above 90, and carried more than 8st 12lbs.

The key to this puzzle is distance. 7/10 winners had not won over the distance, but had done so over 10f, 4 of them in their previous race (LIFT AND LOAD 1990; TORCHON 1991; LEARMONT 1993; HERITAGE 1997). This suggests that they are improving 3 year olds which require a longer distance. If you are prepared to look in the dark for this type of horse, then this is a good handicap for those with night vision. A 'possibles' race par excellence.

There aren't many winners that have won handicaps last time out over the distance, but they are always worth considering:

1996 SAMRAAN   -1 Dunlop   Newbury W 14-1
1998 DOUBLE CLASSIC -4 Stoute   Goodwood W 4-1f

Winners of this race often seem to fall into a rather awkward category for their owners: rather high in the handicap to win, but not quite good enough to score in Listed company.

However, if they can be placed in another handicap, there is another problem: their age. As three year olds, they may be a little young to test against their elders if they run again quite soon. The results of the all-aged Old Newton Cup, run two weeks later, give some support to this idea. Both LEARMONT (1993) and HERITAGE (1997) were beaten in that race. MIDNIGHT LEGEND (1994) was wisely confined to his age group when winning at the July Goodwood meeting (9-2f).

Royal Hunt Cup 8f handicap
Age: 9/10 were 4 or 5 y o s; 1/65 runners of other ages
Rating: no pattern

This is an impossibly tricky handicap. In the 1990s, 5 winners of this race had weak or non-existent form credentials. Two (1991 EUROLINK THE LAD, 1995 REALITIES) had not won during this season ; two had not previously won a handicap (1993 IMPERIAL BALLET; 1997 RED ROBBO); and one had not run that season (1992 COLOUR SERGEANT). Only one (1998 REFUSE TO LOSE) had won over the distance during the season. No penalised winner has been successful since 1985, a sign that recent handicap form is not relevant.

For the more speculative punter looking for 'possible' winners, there are some definite trends. Insofar as it is ever won by horses with any or recent form, the race goes to winners at 7f. Both FACE NORTH (1994) and YEAST (1996) won the Victoria Cup, and SHOWBOAT (1999) won a 7f Newmarket handicap. The race is often won by the leading trainers, who like to have a tilt at this race given the prize money on offer (£69,600 prize money in 2000), but it is not easy to see any pattern in their preparation.

The winners between 1990-1999 went on to contest, in the same season, 22 handicaps, for a fairly modest return of four wins. Three of these wins were in the rather average 8f handicap at Ascot at the end of July (PONTENUOVO 1990, COLOUR SERGEANT 1992, and YEAST 1996) and only

PONTENUOVO won another big handicap in the same year (a 7f handicap at Ascot, end of September).

Wokingham 6f handicap

Age: 3 y o s have not won since 1987; 5 y o s have a slight edge
Rating: 8/10 were rated 88+ The most unpredictable race of the whole Royal meeting. If I could persuade you to avoid betting on just one handicap, this would be the one.

For a straight 6f race with an uphill finish, you might expect that races at Newmarket or Sandown would be targetted as a suitable preparation, but winners from those courses very rarely attempt this race. Form and class are no guides, as 7 of the last 10 winners (to 2000) had not won during the season. More than any other handicap at the Royal Ascot meeting this is often won by a trainer not quite out of the top drawer. Despite its apparently competitive nature it may have become rather a weak race, which probably reflects the depressed state of the metropolitan handicaps. SELHURSTPARK FLYER won off 94 in 1997 and repeated this achievement in 1998 off 100, the first dual winner since 1933. The race is also difficult to evaluate as a form guide. It usually has a bearing on the Stewards' Cup, Goodwood, but exactly what bearing is not clear. About half the winners here try to win at Goodwood, but the overwhelming majority find it difficult to follow up. In the 25 years to 1999, only three were successful (CALIBINA 1977, PETONG 1984, KNIGHT OF MERCY 1990). I have checked the winning times carefully, and although CALIBINA and KNIGHT OF MERCY scored in fast times, PETONG recorded a slowish time, as did many Wokingham winners who lost at Goodwood. It is probably more profitable to look at the placed horses. LAW COMMISSION (1994) ran very well here, just failing to get up. However, by the time he ran in the Stewards' Cup, he still had not won a handicap, so he could be discounted.

LOCHSONG (1992) is a good example of running well from a bad draw. The first six home were drawn 29, 28, 21, 17 (LOCHSONG), 24, 23, so she had run much better than her placing suggested. She went on to win the Stewards Cup in good style.

DANETIME (1997) narrowly failed to win, under possibly an injudicious ride from a U.S. jockey. He then won well at Newmarket (6f) before taking the Stewards Cup.

ASCOT FESTIVAL

The Ascot Festival at the end of September was introduced because the centre of gravity of the non-handicap season had moved towards October onwards. These handicaps are well endowed with prize money.

The meeting does not quite attract the standard of runners one might expect given all the attempts at promoting a relatively new fixture. There are two problems: it falls at slightly an awkward point in the programme, just before the two big Newmarket meetings; and is affected by the autumnal equinox, which often means stormy weather, heavy rain and rapidly changeable going. In the last ten years the going throughout the meeting has been good to firm only twice (1996 and 1997); was 'heavy' once (1999); and has been soft or good to soft in the other years.

There are three big handicaps at this meeting: the Mile Final Handicap (8f); the Tote 7f; and the Ritz Club 12f.

Mile Final Handicap
Age: no pattern, except that only 1/39 3 y o s have been successful
Rating: no pattern

If the statistical trends are confusing, so is the form record.

Although the top weight is usually rated around 100, making this a handicap of reasonable quality, the race has been won by some weak horses, the last four being rated 74, 74, 74 and 70. In the 1990s, this handicap was only won once by a leading trainer, Sir Michael Stoute with SELAAH in 1991. Typically the winner had shown no previous form at all, since he was unplaced in his only races during the season.

Ritz Club 12f handicap
Age: no pattern
Rating: 7/10 winners were rated 88 +

The statistical trends are for the most part inconclusive, although they do seem to suggest that this is a race which is becoming more competitive. The major clue is the record of Luca Cumani, whose horses placed in the Ebor or at the Ebor meeting have included the following winners:

1991 Tidemark   W 10-1
1999 Vicious Circle   W 13-2

and two losers, an exceptional feat given that the Ebor is run over two furlongs further.

Tote 7f handicap
Age: 0/9* winner were 6 y o +

Rating: 8/9 were rated 84-96

* the 1999 meeting was abandoned

The statistical indicators are so weak that they do not allow the elimination of many of the runners.

The form record is especially puzzling for this specialist distance. 6 of the 9 winners were successful over the trip during the current season, but of these two had also won over 8 furlongs. Winning form over the distance is not so important as usual. The only form horse to win this race was SHARPALTO in 1992, so for form specialists this is a race best avoided.

But it is definitely a race for 'possibles', proven handicappers who have good recent form, but not over the distance, and from a strong stable (e.g. PONTENUOVO 1990; WIZARD KING 1994; DECORATED HERO 1996).

AYR

A flat, galloping, left-handed course, with well-graded bends leading to a long, 4f run in, this is a very fair test. It has one notable meeting, the Ayr Western Meeting, three days in the middle of September, which is quite well placed between the Doncaster St. Leger meeting and the series of Newmarket meetings in the final weeks of the season. Although there are usually two or three Listed races, the meeting neither has the social prestige to attract owners to compete for the quite modest handicap prizes on offer, nor does it have a series of big handicaps. Nor are the handicaps useful pointers to big handicaps at the end of the season. Over a decade ago the Eglinton and Winton Challenge Cup, run over 2m 1f 105y, was sometimes used as a trial for the Cesarewitch but its status and prize money have plummeted, since in 1999 the prize money was lower than it was in 1984. As an indication of its current weakness, the race was won for three years in a row (1998-2000), by GIVE AN INCH. Unfortunately, the overall strength of the meeting seems to have declined in recent years.

Against this rather discouraging background, the Ayr Gold Cup is one of the best sprint handicaps in the entire season. In the last decade, it has pulled steadily towards and then away from the Wokingham (Royal Ascot) and the Stewards' Cup (Goodwood), to become the richest sprint handicap in Britain.

Ayr Gold Cup 6f handicap

This is a much sought-after prize, so you can expect it to be competitively run. Are there any trends?

Age: 9/10 winners were 3 and 4 y o

Rating: 9/10 winners rated 89 +

The one definite statistical trend - that younger horses win a disproportionate number of times - is in fact confirmed over a much longer period, the last forty years, so you should begin your search among this age group. Most of the pre-race speculation turns on the significance of the draw. It is certainly true that in the 1990s, no winner was drawn in the middle of the field (9-16; the usual field is around 30). When the race is run on soft going, a high draw (28, 29) seems to be the key. On other types of going, the winners have been drawn 17, 8, 24, 28, 27, 8, 18, 8, i.e. 3 drawn towards the low side, 3 definitely on the high side, and 2 near the middle.

Rather than speculate, is it better to look at the Silver Cup, run two races earlier on the same day, as a guide to the draw? In the 2000 race, the first six home were drawn 26, 20, 27, 9, 23, 22 in a 29 runner race. Is this clear evidence of a bias towards runners drawn high? - hardly, as the first six home in the race run one hour and a quarter later, the Gold Cup, were drawn 7, 2, 23, 10, 24, 28, also a 29 runner field. An examination of other years' results will confirm that this plausible suggestion does not work out in practice.

Instead, it makes more sense to look carefully at the form record. Some of the bare facts are intriguing. All 10 of the winners had scored in a 6f or 7f handicap earlier in the season; 6/10 winners were fillies; 3/3 penalised fillies won; and 11/11 penalised colts/geldings lost. On this basis, a fair proportion of the runners can be discounted, but what are the positive signs, i.e. how reliable is the form shown in the other major sprint handicaps?

The Portland Handicap, run at Doncaster one week previously seems a well-placed preparation race. It does not matter that the distance is about 100 yards shorter, because the winner of the earlier race is usually a 6f specialist. But the record shows that it is an unusual double, which was pulled off by SARCITA (1991) and by the exceptional LOCHSONG (1992). Short-termists might think that they have spotted a trend, but in the longer term they are deluded. JONGEORGE (1977) was the last double winner; before that, the double had not been won since before the war; and there has been no subsequent dual success. Unplaced runners from the Portland do not do well: since the last winner Ayr Gold Cup in this category, NOT SO SILLY (1987), 73 runners have tried and failed.

The other obvious pointer is the Stewards' Cup (Goodwood). In the 1990s, 5 winners attempted to carry off the Ayr race, 2 successfully, LOCHSONG (1992) and COASTAL BLUFF (1996). Looking beyond these two handicaps, there is another form pattern. With very rare exceptions (e.g. ROYALE FIGURE in 1995), the winner has won a good 6f or 7f handicap within the last four handicaps. The real key to this race is not the draw but the going. On the west coast of Scotland, even with the warming influence of the Gulf Stream (remember those geography lessons at school), at Ayr 'soft going' or even 'good to soft' means 'soft and wet' and not 'yielding and mildly damp'. When the going is good to soft or worse, the result is utterly unpredictable. The only exception was LOCHSONG (1992), a truly remarkable horse, trained by the equally remarkable I A Balding. Unfortunately, the going is good or firmer only about four times a decade. But in the 1990s, the reward for waiting patiently for the right going was worthwhile:

WILDWOOD FLOWER (1997; won Goodwood 6f) W 14-1
COASTAL BLUFF (1996; won Stewards Cup) W 3-1
SHIKARI'S SON (1995; won Stewards Cup) L 10-1
SARCITA (1991; won Portland) W 14-1

Conversely, runners with good form credentials run badly when the going is good to soft / soft / heavy. In summary, when the going is good or firmer, then form horses have an outstanding record; when it is good to soft or softer, put on your blindfold and reach for the pin. On balance, this is a neutral race, in that it only follows a definite pattern under certain circumstances. The winners of the Gold Cup rarely win another handicap during the season, as they are now quite high in the weights, and there are no big handicaps, so it means carrying a high weight in a moderate handicaps, or going for a stakes race.

CHESTER

A really difficult course, as it is a circle, only just over a mile round, left-handed and completely flat. There are no other courses like it in Britain, although in Ireland there are one or two of a similar shape, such as Galway.

The only major meeting takes place the beginning of May. Although this has two Listed and two Group 3 races, only one handicap, the Chester Cup, is of similar class. Winners of the Cup must count themselves fortunate, as the prize money of £65000 (in 2000) is a great reward for a field of rather ordinary handicappers.

Chester Cup 2m 2f handicap
There are two quite clear statistical trends:
Age: aged horses cannot be ruled out, as two 7 y o s have won
Rating: 9/10 winners were rated 88 or below

The signals from the form trends are rather mixed. The race can be won by a previous winner, as TOP CEES showed in 1995 and, in 1997, the race which put fat fees in the pockets of Messrs Sue, Grabbit and Runne. That three aged horses (RODEO STAR 1993; TOP CEES 1997; SILENCE IN COURT 1998) have been successful is not too surprising, as this age group does quite well in distance handicaps. There is some evidence that it is probably best to look for reasonable form over 2m this season, in the 2m handicaps at Kempton and Newbury, but it is not very conclusive.

DONCASTER

Although overshadowed by York in terms of prestige and prize money, Doncaster is, in my view, far superior. Of British racecourses, it is excelled only by Newmarket; some outstanding judges, such as Barry Hills, even consider it the best. Apart from a small hill 8 furlongs from the finish, the left-handed course is flat throughout, with wide sweeping bends leading to a long run of $4^1/2$ furlongs. York's conformation is just as good, but Doncaster's advantage is derived from its turf, which gives the most perfect surface of any British or Irish racecourse. When it rains, the going does turn soft or even heavy (at the November meeting), but the change takes place quite gradually, and affects all parts of the track. Unlike York, the going does not become unpredictably or unevenly soft, leading to shock results.

There are three important meetings at Doncaster: the Lincoln meeting, which marks the beginning of the Flat, at the end of March; the St. Leger meeting at the beginning of September; and the November meeting, which concludes the Flat season. The meetings between the end of March and the St. Leger meeting are rather ordinary in quality, and neither offer large prize handicaps nor tempt the leading trainers.

THE LINCOLN MEETING

Since Lincoln racecourse was closed in 1964, the Flat racing season begins at Doncaster. Journalists often complain that the season begins rather quietly, and it is true that in terms of prize money there are no big handicaps. But leading trainers occasionally use this meeting to place horses which showed improved form at the end of the previous season.

The Lincoln 8f handicap
Age: no pattern
Rating: 8/10 were rated 87 or less
The Lincoln is the first big handicap of the season, worth over £43000 in 2001. Since there is no current form, this is a very unpredictable race, as shown by the SP of the winners. In the last decade, there have been 8 long-priced winners (2 at 33-1, 2 at 22-1, 4 at 16-1), these prices being, if anything, an optimistic reflection of their form chance. If it is difficult to predict the result of the Lincoln, the winner's future career is much more clear cut: almost

unrelieved failure. Since 1990 only EVICHSTAR (1990) won a reasonable race later in the same season. In their later races Lincoln winners are only worth considering as a good source of false-priced favourites. Placed horses have a much better record, but not in big handicaps, except for the Newbury Spring Cup. The other handicaps are nowhere near as valuable as the Lincoln but do offer the occasional opportunity. In the first month of the season, the only other big meetings are at Kempton and Newmarket, so if a leading trainer has a runner at this meeting which showed good form at the end of the previous season, look carefully at its chances. For example, in 1998 TURN-POLE (Mrs. Reveley) won the 2m 2f handicap at this meeting after winning the Cesarewitch. The Spring Mile is not a valuable race, with a prize money of only £14000, but the winner can often go on to win a similarly modest handicap.

THE ST LEGER MEETING

7f handicap

This handicap is one of the most surprising races in the entire Flat season. It is not worth trying to pick the winner, but to follow the runners which have won in good style, even when not from a leading stable, has been very rewarding. Here is the record:

1990	RISEN MOON (B W Hills)	Cambridgeshire	W 7-1
1991	PERFOLIA (Gosden)	Newmarket 7f	W 11-4f
1991	PERFOLIA (Gosden)	Newmarket 7f	W 5-2f
1994	POLISH ADMIRAL (C F Wall)	Newmarket 7f	W 5-2f
1994	POLISH ADMIRAL (C F Wall)	Newmarket 7f	W 13-2
1996	QUILLING (Dods)	Redcar 7f	W 7-2 FPF
1998	SALTY JACK (V Soane)	Newmarket 7f	W 4-1 FPF

In addition, EN ATTENDANT, the 1992 winner, turned out to be a really capable 7f winner over the next two seasons, winning four 7f handicaps at the July course Newmarket.

Portland 5f 140y handicap

The Portland is not a valuable handicap these days, since the Stewards' Cup carries more than twice the prize money, and recently it has been overtaken in terms of winnings by the Great St Wilfrid. However, it still attracts good quality sprint handicappers because the St Leger meeting is fashionable, and the race is a staging post en route to the Ayr Gold Cup.

Age: 8/10 winners were 3 or 4 y o

Rating: 10/10 were rated 84+

An undue amount of attention is given to the draw, but it does not seem to have any importance.

Sometimes the statistical guidelines are a little less impressive than they seem. In the 2000 race, they only pointed to the elimination of 3 runners out of 22, a not untypical result. Are the form guidelines any more helpful?

Form does work out well in this race. Course-and-distance winners have a good record: AMRON (1993), HELLO MISTER (1994 and 1995), CADEAUX CHER (1998) and ASTONISHED (1999) had all won over the course-and-distance at some previous point in their careers. If there are no such winners, what is the most suitable distance preparation for this race, i.e. will a 5f winner last the extra 140 yards, or will a 6f horse find the course a vital 100 yards too short? 5f horses, such as DASHING BLUE (1997), tend to be able to win when unopposed by good 6f horses, but otherwise, the 6f winners generally have the advantage, as SARCITA (1991) and LOCHSONG (1992) showed.

THE NOVEMBER MEETING

The Flat season stumbles into life at Doncaster, but concludes with a flourish, and the final meeting here must not be missed. The fields are large, as this is Last Chance saloon for many of the runners. Even though the horses don't know that defeat or a poor performance here means an imminent posthumous trip to Belgium, the owners and trainers do, so there are plenty of optimistic entries. Doncaster is a course on the grand scale, and can cope with the resulting large fields. November 12f handicap

Age: 7/10 winners 3 y o s

Rating: 7/10 winners were rated 90+

Three year olds are markedly over-represented with 7 wins from 65 runners, as compared to 3 wins from 157 for the other age groups, but the weight/rating guidelines are not very indicative. Form is a much more useful pointer. Look for distance winners within the last 6 weeks, particularly from Haydock and Newmarket. The only qualifiers with this pattern all won here:

1992 TURGENEV
1994 SAXON MAID
1995 SNOW PRINCESS
1999 FLOSSY

If you look for 'possible' or 'dark' horses, then it is worth noting that 5 of the other winners had also run well during this period at Haydock and Newmarket. The going was good to soft 7 times in the 1990s, so make sure that your selection can handle the going. Lightly-raced three year old fillies do very well in these circumstances.

EPSOM

A left-handed undulating course: uphill for the first 4f, level for about 2f, downhill round Tattenham corner, a further 3f downhill, and then a gentle rise in the final furlong.

A generation ago, Epsom used to stage two major handicaps, the City and Suburban (10f) and the Great Metropolitan (2m 2f). With the demise of the Spring meeting in 1990, these handicaps, which had lost their prize money and their prestige, were not transferred to other courses. When the meeting made a welcome return, in 2001, someone at the bookmakers, Stanley Racing, with a sense of history ensured that there was a City and Suburban (10f) and a Great Metropolitan Stakes (12f). Unfortunately, the prize money was only £11,500 and £15,000 respectively. The handicaps at the new meetings in July and August are poor affairs, and not worth considering.

The one big meeting at Epsom, the Derby meeting, is of no interest to the handicap specialist, despite the fairly good prize money on offer. On Derby day in 1999, the winners of the handicaps were rewarded with £24900 (12f) £31940 (10f), and £25305 (6f); and on Oaks Day, £18156 (6f). Tempting enough, you might think, especially given the incessant, if justified, complaints by owners about the low level of prize money; and run on two of the most socially prestigious days in the racing calendar.

So why do these handicaps not attract good enough horses to fall into the category of big handicaps? At various times, most of the leading trainers have stated that, apart from the Derby and the Oaks, they are reluctant to bring their runners here because of the nature of the course. Many good horses who do well elsewhere completely fail to act when trying to negotiate Tattenham corner. It is hard to prepare for Epsom because there is no other top class course with a similar conformation.

GOODWOOD

Goodwood is in effect three courses: a straight 6f course, with an uphill start; and the two loops onto the dog-leg course for various distances from 7f to 2m 4f. The sprint course favours the relentless galloper; while well-balanced handy types of classic conformation do well at the other distances. The quality of the turf, laid out in the 1840s on a chalk subsoil, is second only to Doncaster. It usually drains very quickly, but rather unevenly, so be careful when the going changes to soft.

Most of the big handicaps are concentrated at the 5 day July meeting, although there are good quality, if not lavishly rewarded handicaps at the August and September meetings. At the July meeting, which usually gives one or two good opportunities every year, there is a simple form rule which renders elaborate statistical analysis unnecessary, i.e. only to consider recent winners from Ascot, Newmarket or Sandown. The one exception is:

The Stewards' Cup 6f handicap
Age: 8/10 winners were 4 y o s
Rating: 8/10 rated 91-100

The statistical record is helpful in terms of weight and rating, but misleading about age. On the face of it the three year old record of one winner from 51 runners is dreadful. But it is asking a lot for a three year old sprinter to compete against older horses at the end of July, as they really come to hand later in the season. When there is an improving three year old from a top stable, then you do have a chance. It is true that this might only be once in a decade: DANETIME (1997, Callaghan); AUTUMN SUNSET (1983, Stoute).

There are two additional trends, not very clear cut: 2/10 winners penalised, both carrying a 7 pounds penalty; 2 winners came here after a good run in the Wokingham.

The rule about Ascot winners does not seem to apply to this race. In particular, about half of the winners of the Wokingham try to win this race, but the overwhelming majority find it difficult to follow up. In the period 1975-99, only three of the twenty-five winners of the Wokingham were successful here (CALIBINA 1977, PETONG 1984, KNIGHT OF MERCY 1990). I have checked the winning times carefully. Although CALIBINA and KNIGHT OF MERCY scored in fast times, Ascot winners in fast times, such as TIME MACHINE (1985) lost here, while the other double scorer, PETONG, won in a slow time winner. It might be more rewarding to look carefully at the placed horses. LOCHSONG (1992) ran well from a bad draw at Ascot, while DANETIME (1997) was an unlucky loser.

To sum up this difficult, but soluble race. In most years, the right form combination does not exist, so a 'shock' result is inevitable when a horse with no recent form comes good on the day.

HAYDOCK

Racing is nowhere near as popular as football on this side of the Pennines which perhaps explains why such a splendid racecourse has only rather average handicaps. Haydock is an excellent galloping course, 13f round, left-handed, with a slight but steady rise throughout the final straight four furlongs.

The Old Newton Cup 12f handicap

Haydock's one major Flat handicap is the 12f Old Newton Cup. The race comes at just the right interval after the two 12f handicaps at Royal Ascot, the Duke of Edinburgh and the King George V. However, in the last decade fewer of the leading trainers have aimed their Ascot winners at this race than in the past. In fact, the only two were HERITAGE and ZARALASKA, which both contested the 1995 race, with the latter coming out on top. In 1983, this race was twice as valuable as its Ascot equivalents; by the end of the 1990s, all three handicaps were roughly equal. This decline in the value of the Cup may explain why it is no longer so attractive to Ascot winners.

KEMPTON

There are two courses here. The right-handed 'round' course is triangular in shape, with sharp bends leading to a 3 Ωf run in; the Jubilee course is a dog-leg, curving gently to the left, then turns to the right into the run in.

For London racegoers, Kempton's decline is a matter of great regret. The Easter meeting used to see the (re) appearance of good class handicappers. The Rosebery (10f) was a good race for horses which had won in high class in the previous season. SPECIAL DAWN, trained by John Dunlop, fell into this category twice, winning in 1995 and losing in 1996. The canny P W Harris trained AMERICAN WHISPER to repeat the pattern in 1998, but with prize money of just under £22,000, the race has fallen into such a precipitous decline that its effective abolition (run as a nondescript 8f handicap in 2000) passed without comment in the press. In 2001 its original distance was re-established, but the prize money, though high for the meeting, was still only £23,000. The Jubilee 8f handicap (May meeting) used to be the Great Jubilee Handicap, first staged in 1887, and important enough to give its name to one of Kempton's courses. Although the prize money of £29,180 in 1999 was mildly tempting at this point of the season, it has ceased to attract the better class handicappers. If you must bet in this race, look carefully at course and distance winners, as in the 1990s the race was won twice by repeat winners, DESERT GREEN (1995, 1996) and TERTIUM (1998, 1999).

NEWBURY

Newbury has a brand new stand, designed by an architectural knight (Foster) - but hardly matched by the calibre of the racing. Its decline as a Flat venue is difficult to explain: it is very convenient for the major training centres in Berkshire and Wiltshire; the turf is of excellent quality; and the course layout is fair and testing. It is a 15f left-handed oval, mainly flat, with slight undulations on the straight 5f run-in.

Its programme includes a neatly spaced series of Cups: Spring (8f), Summer (12f), and Autumn (1m 5f 61y), in April, June and September. The Spring Cup used to attract some attention and reasonable fields because it was the first big 8f handicap after the Lincoln, but in the last decade its status has gradually declined. If you must bet in this race, look carefully at the placed horses in the Lincoln, or the winner of the Spring Mile at the same meeting. The Summer Cup used to be a useful trial for Royal Ascot, but no longer; and the Autumn Cup, once a follow-up race for winners at the Doncaster St Leger meeting, is now a very ordinary handicap indeed.

The Highclere Nursery (September) used to be a good trial for the end of season handicaps, but seems to have sunk without trace in the last few years.

NEWCASTLE

A left-handed oval, 14f round, with a 4f run in.

Newcastle is 100 miles on the wrong side of the North-South divide in racing. Further south, its merits would be widely recognised, as it is a very testing track, with a gruelling uphill finish, and form shown in reasonable quality races is thoroughly reliable. It is an undeservedly neglected course, but it is to be hoped that Stan Clarke can revive its fortunes.

Northumberland Plate 2m 192y handicap
Age: 6/10 4 y o s
Rating: 8/10 winners rated 85+

The statistics tell no sort of story at all, and unfortunately neither does the form. There have been strange winners of this race, and in the 1990s, three of the winners had not previously won during the season, usually an indicator of a race in which form is at a discount.

This is the kind of distance race which attracts the attention of Martin Pipe, and in the 1990s he won with two runners out of four (TAMARPOUR 1991; FAR CRY 1999). In that decade, only two winners had good recent form over the distance: WITNESS BOX (1992) had scored at Newmarket, and was trained by the inevitable John Gosden; and FAR CRY had won at Kempton. When owners and trainers realise that the prize money is now (from 2000) comparable to that of the Cesarewitch, the result may be more competitive fields of good class handicappers.

NEWMARKET

Newmarket is not a course for 'dark' or 'possible' horses: form reigns supreme. The wide, galloping courses (the July course and the Rowley Mile) with their relentless uphill finishes; the large, competitive fields, which usually include several runners from the leading stables; the prestige for owners of winning a race at 'Headquarters': all these factors add up to make Newmarket the top form course.

With the exception of the Cambridgeshire, course and distance form is absolutely essential. Remember that although both courses share the same general characteristics, the July course is even more testing than the Rowley Mile, and form between the two is not transferable. There are two outstanding handicaps at Newmarket, the Cambridgeshire and the Cesarewitch; and numerous handicaps of good quality, though often poorly rewarded. Among the latter type, I would like to single out those run over 7f.

7f handicaps

This is a specialists' distance, too far for the sprinters, too short for the middle-distance runners. At Newmarket, the peculiarities of the course make previous course and distance form absolutely essential. There is a neatly spaced series of 7f races throughout the season, which give enough opportunities to these specialist runners. The advantage of being a specialist is so great that, exceptionally for Newmarket, it is not necessary to concentrate on the leading stables. In the last decade, the results of races in which course-and-distance winners have been the form selection are as follows:

1991	PERFOLIA	W 5-2f
1992	HOB GREEN	W 13-2
1993	EN ATTENDANT	W 11-1
1994	POLISH ADMIRAL	W 13-2
1995	CADEAUX TRYST	L 7-1
1996	ALMUHIMM	L 4-1f
1996	CRUMPTON HILL	L 7-1
1999	CRUINN A BORD	W 7-1
1999	KARAMEG	L 7-1jf

Oddly enough, the 7f handicap which carries the highest prize money (£26000 in 2000), the Bunbury Cup, run at the first July meeting, should usually be avoided, as the following analysis shows.

Bunbury Cup 7f handicap July course
Age: 8/10 were 3 and 4 y o s, and this age group has a proportionally (8% of runners) better record than older horses (2%)
Rating: 9/10 rated 85+

The rating statistics suggest that this race goes to an exposed handicapper. But the results show that this is not a form race. Distance winners do not have a very good record, since only 4 of the last 10 winners had been successful over the distance in the same season, and 6 of the winners had not won any race during the season. Exceptionally, course and distance winners have a poor record or have no recent form. For example, the course specialist EN ATTENDANT won this race for the second time, in 1994, with seasonal form figures of 00. In all, half of the 1990 winners had yet to score during the season, and only four had won at the distance in their year. Reluctantly, because this is a high betting turnover race at a smart meeting, the Bunbury has to be written off as 'trappy'.

Cambridgeshire 9f handicap Rowley Mile
Age: 0/71 5 y o runners won; no other pattern
Rating: 8/9* rated 93 or below
*The 1999 race was run on the July course over 10f

The statistical record gives no clues, and at first sight, it seems unlikely that on form grounds it would be possible to select the winner of the Cambridgeshire with any confidence. The 9f trip is unusual, as there are no handicaps at either Newmarket course over this distance; at the big meetings elsewhere, there are minor 9f handicaps at Goodwood and York. It is a very tough race, a straight 9f ending in an uphill finish, with a big field usually charging off at a shattering pace. Yet there are a number of key form indicators which help point the way. The winners have usually won at 7f, 8f and 10f, but not, curiously enough, over 9f, at a leading course (Ascot, Doncaster, Newbury, York). The Doncaster St Leger meeting is a good source of candidates. Winners of the 10f race were: SUE'S ARTISTE (1994 L 11-1); HALLING (1994 W 8-1); and CLIFTON FOX (1996 W 14-1). In a longer perspective, both winners of the 7f handicap entered for this race have won (TREMBLANT 1985; RISEN MOON 1990). The race is usually won by one of the big stables, although the extremely shrewd but unfashionable stable of Jeremy Glover has won three times, with RAMBO'S HALL (1989, 1992) and CLIFTON FOX (1996).

Cesarewitch 2m 2f handicap Rowley Mile
Age: 6 y o s have the best strike rate (5-80)
Rating: no pattern

If there is no pattern in the statistical record, the form signals are also quite confusing. At one time, this was a good race for a lightly raced 3 year old or 4 year old which had won around 2m. Not any more, as in the last decade only TRAINGLOT (1990) followed that pattern. The Cesarewitch now seems to be a race for well exposed older handicappers. Since 1991, four winners (including TOP CEES 1999, when the race was run over the July course) have been 7 years old and over. Although these winners have quite a long racing history, their form record is not very clear, as 4/10 winners had not won over 14f or longer during the current season.

REDCAR

A long, narrow, left-handed oval.

Although the bends leading to the 5f run in are rather tight, this is generally a good galloping course. Two handicap races, the Zetland Gold Cup and the Vaux Gold Tankard appear more for the historic record than for their current interest.

The Zetland Gold Cup (10f, end of May) used to fill an early season gap in the programme for races of this distance, and has been won by horses with form shown at good class courses (FRIDU 1988, INAAD 1989, ERADICATE 1990, WAINWRIGHT 1994, MIGWAR 1996, and CHAMPAGNE PRINCE 1997). However the prize money has more than halved in money terms, from £24,000 in 1990 to £11,000 in 2000.

A generation ago, the Vaux Gold Tankard (10f, end of June) was endowed with the same prize money as the Ebor, but by 1996 the prize money had fallen to £14,000 and then to its current level of £8700, a fate it has shared with other 10f handicaps. But since form works out well on this course, if a big handicap or two was added to the programme, to complement the 2 year old stakes race at the end of September, they would be well worth considering.

SANDOWN

A 13f oval, right-handed course. The straight 4f run in, and the long uphill finish, sort out the unreliable horses and make this a course for form horses. The separate 5f course is uphill all the way.

Races on the sprint course are rather difficult to see, but otherwise the excellent grandstand offers the best viewing position on any British racecourse.

Sandown has retained the prestige of its non-handicap races, but its handicaps have gone into a spiral of decline in the last five years or so.

The Esher Cup (8f 3yo April), at a useful pointer in the season for late-developing horses in their second season, seems to have vanished without trace. Likewise, the Whitsun Cup (8f all-aged), celebrating a public holiday and the beginning of summer, has been ignominiously retitled the Doubleprint Rated Stakes, and is currently of no consequence.

The first meeting in July used to have one big handicap, over 10f, the Royal Hong Kong Jockey Club. Often the insular world of racing can ignore the outside world. There hasn't been a Tsarevitch since 1918, but the Cesarewitch is still an important handicap, and the Coal Miners handicap continues to be run at Doncaster, surviving the industry after which it was named. But the Royal Hong Kong Jockey Club handicap lost the prefix Royal and then, in 2000, seems to have metamorphosed into the less exotic Tote Exacta Stakes. True it is unduly sentimental to regret the loss of a title if the handicap continues to be a competitive one, but in this case the first running of this once hotly-competitive race under its new name seems to suggest further decline. The winner, LADY ANGHARAD, had not previously won a handicap.

YORK

A left-handed 13f oval, flat throughout. A racecourse on the grand scale, with wide sweeping turns leading to a 5f run in, it has one major flaw: unpredictable going. When it rains, the course does not drain evenly or quickly. The going changes so quickly that you need to know the state of the turf immediately before the off, not†on the morning of the race. I have learnt the expensive way that you should avoid betting at York unless the sun is shining and the going is good or faster.

Although the general level of handicap racing is quite good, for the big handicap specialist, only two handicaps are worth considering in detail: the John Smith's Cup (mid-July) and the Ebor (the August meeting). In both cases, the going has been good or faster in 9 years out of 10, so that York's major flaw is not exposed.

Ebor Handicap 1m 6f handicap

As Yorkshiremen will proudly tell you, this race 'is worth a bob or two'. Although they are also inclined to call the Royal Ascot meeting, 'the York of the South', in this case they are right. Unlike some big handicaps, it has increased its value in the last two years, to become the richest staying race (i.e. including non-handicaps) in Europe. This is a complicated handicap to analyse, as the trends are not immediately obvious. But it is worth doing so, as if you can find a selection, there is tremendous value to be obtained in the very strong betting market.

Age: 3yo s have the best strike rate (4 winners, 12.5%), as compared to 3% for 4 yos (3 winners) and 7.5% for 5 yos (3 winners).
Rating: no pattern

Draw: for once there is a discernible pattern, that 9/10 winners were drawn 1-10. The longer term record (the 20 years up to and including 1999) shows that there are 3 persistent trends. The top stables have a good record (9 winners), but do not dominate this race as they do some of the Royal Ascot handicaps. On the other hand, the race has only rarely (twice) been won by stables which never win big handicaps. Three year olds have a good record, winning 9 times, while there were no 6 y o winners. The record of the draw was available for 15 years only, and during this period 13 winners were drawn 1-10. The form profile is either a lightly-raced three year old, making his way up the handicap or an experienced, but not over exposed older horse. But this is still very much a race for 'dark horses', as the winner may have been successful over a longer distance (FURTHER FLIGHT 1990), over 12f (QUICK RANSOM 1992, SANMARTINO 1995); 13f (PRIMARY 1986) or even 10f (VICIOUS CIRCLE 1999). The winner may not even have a won a handicap (CRAZY 1984, KNELLER 1988; SANMARTINO 1995; CLERKENWELL 1996). This is a difficult race, but if you can find the combination of form profile/top-class trainer/draw/'dark horse', which seems to come up about 3 or 4 times a decade, then you are on to something. To repeat the advice given above, if the going is soft, do not bet however appealing a combination you see.

John Smith's Cup 10f handicap
Age: 6 y o s at a disadvantage, since the last winner was in 1969
Rating: 6/10 winners rated 90+

This is not an easy race to assess. The statistical guidelines are somewhat uninformative, and the form record is rather mixed. In 4 years out of 10, the winner had either not won a handicap or not won any kind of race in the current season. On the other hand, the race has been won by good handicappers which have already set up a sequence, such as ERADICATE (1990), CEZANNE (1994) and PASTERNAK (1997). The absolutely top flight trainers have very few runners in this event. Typically, Henry Cecil won with PORTO FORICOS (1998), an easy winner of a 9f maiden at Goodwood. Given the glittering prize, of £87,000, it is surprising to see how dim the runners often are.

FLAT RACING IN IRELAND

Until very recently, it was fairly difficult for anyone living in the U.K. to follow handicap racing in Ireland. The handicap marks were only published in the Turf Club's Racing Calendar, but the Racing Post has done a wonderful job in remedying this deficiency. However, the form is often only available in the first edition of the Post, which is hard to get outside the big cities. But if you have access to the Internet, all the information you require is available on the Racing Post website (www.racingpost.co.uk) or the Irish racing website (www.irishfield.com).

Handicap racing on the Flat in Ireland is nowhere near as competitive as National Hunt. However, the situation may change quite rapidly in the next few years. The Irish government gives much more support to Flat racing and the bloodstock business than its U.K. counterpart. It has effected a transformation in greyhound prize money in the last couple of years, and could well do the same for Flat racing. If it does, and if the competitiveness of Flat handicaps improves, this will be very good news for the backer, since the main Irish courses, Leopardstown and The Curragh are both very good in terms of conformation and layout. At the moment, however, handicap racing is only of consistently reasonable quality at The Curragh.

THE CURRAGH

A big, right-handed 16f round course, with easy turns leading to a 3f run in. Races up to 8f start on a spur, running at an angle to the main course. The straight mile rises by 29 feet, the greatest rise on any British or Irish course. The combination of such a steep uphill finish and a wide course gives the strong runner every chance of success.

The sprint handicaps here, including the quite valuable Scurry handicaps (6f 63y) run in June, are difficult to solve, because there isn't enough previous form over the distance. All the handicaps over a mile and further are worth considering, even though the prize money is unrewarding, because the races are eagerly competed for. Two named handicaps should be considered. The Irish Cambridgeshire, run over a mile in September, frequently falls to a course and distance winner, for example, THE BOWER (1995, 1996).

The Cesarewitch, over 2m in October, has a good record for course and distance winners, and can be won by an aged (7 years and older) horse. For example, MILTONFIELD won this race twice, as well as one other handicap over the course and distance.

★★★
ALL-WEATHER RACING

A.-W. racing is much derided by many racing enthusiasts. True, the sand track lies like a scar across the once pretty face of Lingfield; for a midwinter meeting at Southwell, 'grisly' competes with 'bleak' as the first adjective to come to mind; and boisterous, floodlit Wolverhampton is more like a greyhound track, far removed from the Sport of Kings.

But this type of racing is here to stay, not just as a substitute in periods of bad weather. Form generally works out well, and the backer has priceless information, not available for any other kind of British/Irish racing, in the shape of reliable race times. Race times give an objective measure of performance, but remember that the figures which you need are given in the small print of the form. The Racing Post speed figures are different, since they are calculated to make an allowance for weight.

Unfortunately there is only one big handicap. However, the owners of the A.W. tracks are furlongs ahead of most other racecourse managements in promoting the sport, and it is always possible that big handicaps with good prizes may one day be introduced. So for future reference, I have included a brief section on the two tracks more likely to have better racing in years to come. If you would like to know more, I recommend David Bellingham's Gold From the Sand (Raceform 2000) as a sound introduction.

A decade of A.-W racing has given some clues. The effect of the draw, which I mistakenly discounted in my previous book Bigger Profits from Handicap Races, is significant at some distances and some tracks. Apart from the differences in course layout, the surfaces are different: Lingfield is Equitrack; Southwell and Wolverhampton are Fibresand.

LINGFIELD

The Ladbroke All-Weather Trophy Handicap over 7f mid January is usually a very competitive race by any standards. For instance, in 2001 eight of the 11 strong field had won over the course and distance, and of these three had recent winning form. Unfortunately, it is competition at too low a level (the top mark was 82) for too meagre a reward (just over £10,000) to make it into the big handicap league.

WOLVERHAMPTON

Like Southwell, the track surface is Fibresand. The oval circuit is only 7 Ω furlongs round, with a short run in of 2 furlongs. Over the longer races (from 7f upwards), it is usually necessary to be a quick starter. Given a fast start, neither front runners nor late finishers have a particular advantage. The horses drawn in the middle (3-7) seem to have a slight advantage.

The Lincoln Trial over $8^1/2f$ is the most valuable All Weather handicap, with a prize of £32,500 to the winner in 2001. It is a reasonable trial for the first major Flat handicap, but it is difficult to find the winner of this race. There are not enough years for trend analysis to give any form/statistics clues, but first impressions suggest that it is rather a tricky race. The problem is that, in terms of prize money, the Lincoln Trial is an isolated peak among the lowlands of everyday All-Weather racing. It is as if you were asked to tackle Ben Nevis, when your usual walk was no more than a gentle stroll to the shops. If the All-Weather programme was more balanced in its distribution of prize money (and, of course, had a larger amount to distribute), then this race might follow a pattern, particularly in relation to other races.

If big handicaps can be solved, what is the best approach to doing so?

★★★

THE LEADING TRAINERS

This section analyses the record of those trainers who regularly win the big handicaps. There are no surprises in this list, except perhaps of omission. The omissions are not meant as an indirect criticism of trainers who do not appear on the list. They simply reflect the fact that for some highly successful trainers of big handicaps, I cannot see a pattern in the way they operate.

In two cases, T D Easterby and Mrs Reveley, I make a general point about training methods, so their names are included in brackets below. The trainers on the following list can be relied to win a big handicap or two almost every year.

I A Balding
L Cumani
H R A Cecil
J L Dunlop
(T D Easterby)
J H M Gosden
B W Hills
(Mrs Reveley)
Sir Michael Stoute

D K Weld

To illustrate how I decipher trainers' methods, I have decided to concentrate on the list given above. In many respects, it is best if you draw up your own lists of trainers to follow, so if you read the rest of this chapter together with the advice on how to weigh up a handicap, you will easily be able to do so.

I A Balding

Most of the big trainers do not retain older horses, as their stables would then become impossibly large. Ian Balding is an exception, as he has a good record in big handicaps with older horses such as the 7 y o KNOCK KNOCK, winner of a 10f handicap at the Goodwood July meeting in 1993; and TOP CEES, a 10 year old when he won the 1999 Cesarewitch). Unlike most of the other trainers, he has a keen interest in sprint handicaps winning the Stewards Cup in 1992 (LOCHSONG), the Portland handicap in 1992 (LOCHSONG) and 1997 (DASHING BLUE) and the Ayr Gold Cup in 1992 (LOCHSONG) and 1999 (GRANGEVILLE). Not all trainers have the patience to deal with fillies, particularly to give them a light preparation until they are ready to set up a sequence, but Balding is a master of this difficult art.

Always look out for his runners at the Goodwood July meeting, because he usually brings his horses to their best in the Royal Ascot - Goodwood July - York August period. As well as following a well-beaten path, Balding gives carefully considered comments to the press, including a balanced appraisal of his runners' strengths and weaknesses, and, their likely engagements.

Henry Cecil

Cecil's handicap winners tend to be the classic type of 'dark horse'. They often turn out to be Listed class horses, and winning a big handicap is just one step towards higher things. Even Cecil occasionally cannot work miracles, so some of his handicap geese just are...geese. Without inside information, how are you going to know?

The answer is, that you can have to make an educated guess, on the basis of his past performance. An analysis of his record shows that in the years 1985-99 he won the Britannia Stakes, Royal Ascot twice (from 5 runners) and the Ebor, York August twice (from 4 runners). But there is no way of distinguishing between the winners and the losers in terms of their preparatory races. On the other hand, to pick 4 winners from 9 runners in such competitive races is a good record. And I wonder if Henry Cecil knows what a sprint handicap is?

Luca Cumani

Cumani specialises in the middle-distance handicappers (8f-12f) often well-bred, lightly raced types which if they had a bit more talent would be aimed at Group races. He is one of the three Flat trainers (the other two being John Dunlop and John Gosden) who knows his horses going preferences so well that you do not need to check their previous record.

Unfortunately for this extremely talented trainer, his career has gone round in a circle. He began by training handicappers, and then moved on to Listed/Group winners, but for various reasons his current string mainly consists of handicappers. There is no doubt that he will move on again, but in the meantime make the most of his handicap skills.

John Dunlop

Of all the trainers listed here, John Dunlop has probably the best all-round talent in training handicappers to win races big and small. Any of his horses which have talent work their way methodically from maiden races to small to big handicaps, and he can keep a horse developing like this over a year or two. In particular he is a very good trainer of lightly-raced three year olds, especially fillies. This type of horse often sets up a sequence of wins, leading to success in big handicaps. All the inmates of his stable have to earn their corn, so if any horse is kept on after four years, this is a sign that he is expected to be capable of winning a race. The one type of winner rarely to be found in his stable is the sprint handicapper - EMERGING MARKET, the winner of the 1996 Wokingham, was very much the exception. Dunlop knows when a horse will act on the going, and his comments in the press before big race handicaps are remarkably frank and very informative. Punters ignore them (and they often do) at their cost.

As a trainer of big handicap winners, he is second only to John Gosden. Dunlop's follows the most transparent methods of any of the leading stables, and rarely has 'dark horses'.

T D Easterby

A lion in the north, but a chameleon in the south where his horses do win big handicaps, but not in any very predictable way. In the north he places his handicap winners carefully and systematically, rather in the same manner as his father, M H (Peter) Easterby. This is not intended as a criticism of his methods, but as a reflection on the north-south divide in racing. Even the best northern trainers find it difficult to judge the competition south of the Trent.

J H M Gosden

Quite simply, Gosden is the best trainer under both codes for the big handicaps. He is so good that you could probably make a profit simply by backing every one of his runners in this type of race.

He is a classic case of how quickly a trainer can establish himself in the leading ranks. There was no fluke about his rise to success: his father ('Towser') was also a clever handicap trainer, and he spent several years of apprenticeship in various stables around the world.

He can both produce 'dark horses' and organise a campaign for the form horse. Almost all his winners are middle distance horses, though in an earlier period he did win the Stewards Cup with KING'S SIGNET (1993) and the Northumberland Plate with WITNESS BOX (1992). He knows when his runners will be suited to the ground, and says so in the racing press. Even the best trainers can lose form if they move stables, so it was a relief to see that Gosden's record was unaffected by his move from Newmarket to Manton in 2000.

R Hannon

Unlike most of the other trainers in this list, Hannon does not always have the most plutocratic owners. Unusually he buys in runners from other stables, and is likely to have an unsuccessful horse gelded. He is a very hardworking trainer whose runners cannot be overlooked in the big handicaps. If he has a speciality, it is with sprint handicappers. He won the Wokingham-Stewards Cup double with KNIGHT OF MERCY in 1990, and the Ayr Gold Cup with WILDWOOD FLOWER in 1997. However, a word of caution is needed here. He often has several runners in sprint handicaps, some of which (e.g. BRAVE EDGE, VENTURE CAPITALIST) seem to run more than once in the same race, but only those with good recent form should be considered. Hannon also wins at the 7f and 8f distances, but rarely beyond.

B.W. Hills

Barry Hills set himself up as a trainer with the proceeds of a massive gamble in the Lincoln handicap, over 30 years ago. He continues to be a successful backer, on the basis of very astute placing of his runners to win all kinds of races, big and small. His methods are an instructive contrast with those of, say, John Dunlop. Rather than gradually making their way up the handicap, it seems that his runners are held back from the racecourse until they can make a sudden rush from obscurity to the racing heights. His Ebor winner, SANMARTINO (1995), and the winner of the 1990 Cambridgeshire, RISEN MOON, were both of this kind. His record with the lesser handicaps at the big meetings is rather mixed. It also has to be said that his Royal Ascot winners are the most difficult to anticipate.

Mrs. Reveley

What I have written about T D Easterby (see above) applies to a certain extent about Mrs Reveley: it is often difficult for northern trainers to assess the competition in the big handicaps in the south.

However, Mrs Reveley is successful with one type of horse: the older, distance handicapper. Perhaps because she is a successful dual purpose trainer, there are usually one or two runners in her stable which can win under both codes. Always look carefully at her runners in distance handicaps.

Sir Michael Stoute

Sir Michael Stoute made his mark as a handicap trainer with the sprinter, BLUE CASHMERE, in the early 1970s. Currently his handicap strength lies in middle-distance horses, which tend to be trained in a certain way for particular meetings. He tends to focus on three meetings: Royal Ascot, Goodwood July, and York August. For the big handicaps at Ascot, his runners are very lightly raced 'dark horses' with only one or two preparation races, not always in a handicap. At Goodwood, particularly the Tote Gold Trophy (a 12f race for 3 y os), he has proved adept at producing 'possibles', i.e. handicap winners running on well over a shorter distance. At York, his runners, particularly in the Ebor, tend to be quite well exposed.

However, two words of caution should be noted. His big handicap winners are often successful in Listed races, but are not as successful at winning another big handicap when they might be expected to do so. And, except for the races mentioned above, his stakes winners do not immediately make the transition to handicaps at the first time of asking.

D K Weld

The most successful Flat trainer in the history of Irish Flat racing, and also a very good trainer of National Hunt horses. His runners do well at The Curragh, but his record is best under both codes at the Galway meetings in August and September. He runs some 'dark horses' at the August meeting, but this is hardly news to Irish racegoers, so, whether they are really fancied by the trainer or not, these runners always go off at short prices. Usually these winners have had a previous win or two at the minor courses, such as Gowran Park or Killarney.

The above list does not include trainers who are perfectly capable of winning big handicaps, but do so on a less regular basis. With no implication that they are any the less talented, here is the list of the trainers who can win big handicaps if they have the right material:

J S Bolger (Ireland)
N A Callaghan
D C R Elsworth
P W Harris
K Prendergast (Ireland)
G Wragg

Chapter 4: The big handicaps: National Hunt

In Britain, there are in effect two National Hunt seasons, winter and summer. The winter season in England begins with the Thomas Pink Gold Cup, at Cheltenham on the second weekend of November, and ends at Sandown, with the Whitbread Gold Cup, in the final week of April. It is much more skewed than the Flat, to two major meetings, in March and April: Cheltenham and Aintree.

The National Hunt season is also different in that it has one handicap, the Grand National, which offers a prize about three times greater than the next most valuable handicap. It is such a coveted and rewarding prize (£290,000 in 2000) over a unique distance that there is a whole series of trial races to sort out the leading contenders.

So the National Hunt winter season is like an extended series of rehearsals for only two performances (Aintree and Cheltenham). If you wanted a rest from racing, then you only miss two big handicaps worth betting in (the Hennessy Gold Cup, end of November; the Welsh Grand National, two days after Christmas) if you went abroad and switched off your computer from the beginning of November to the end of January. The season really gets underway in the six weeks leading up to the Cheltenham Festival in March The summer season in England (May to September) has no big handicaps, and given the competition from Flat racing and the strong likelihood of unsuitable going, it is unlikely that this situation will change. In Ireland, there are also two seasons, summer and winter, but both have big handicaps. In summer the softer going on the west coast is favourable to National Hunt racing and the Festival meetings - Galway and Listowel - present some richly endowed handicaps.

The winter season has quite a different character from its British counterpart. Although many of the runners are being trained with Cheltenham in mind, the domestic programme has a much more regular rhythm, with big handicaps at Fairyhouse, Leopardstown and Punchestown.

AINTREE

The Grand National course is perfectly flat, left-handed and over 2m round, an undemanding course. The fences are exactly the opposite. They are enormous, solidly built, and have a marked drop on the landing side. The fences on the Mildmay course (also left-handed) are quite different, as they are like those on an ordinary park course. All the handicaps bar the Grand National and the John Hughes Memorial are run on the Mildmay course.

The Grand National meeting in April has enjoyed a revival in the last five years or so. Although the Grand National has always been popular with the general public, racegoers were beginning to tire of the dismal publicity which surrounded the event and to be uninterested in the supporting card. All this has begun to change. In 2001 it even seemed that Aintree might begin to become a genuine, though friendly rival to Cheltenham. Until then it had become something of a one-race meeting, with prize money and trainers' attention focussed only on the National. The Aintree executive is making serious efforts to arrange a more balanced card, which is all to the good. Because the meeting is changing, a number of the races have not followed a statistical pattern. The soundest form indicator is a win before the Cheltenham Festival, and then a reasonable run (even if as far down as sixth place) at the Festival. Horses which have found either the course or the races there too taxing, find Aintree more congenial.

Cordon Bleu 2m 110yds handicap hurdle

This is a very good example of a race which follows a clear statistical pattern but for which there are no obvious form antecedents. In the last 10 races (to 1999):

Age: 10/10 were aged 5 or 6

Rating: 9/10 winners carried 139 or less

Therefore the pattern is clear enough, but it is of no great help in finding winners. It is not a valuable enough prize to attract Cheltenham runners, as only 3 Cheltenham winners ran in this race in the 1990s, all without distinction. Nor are there any other sources of form winners.

Grand National 4m 4f handicap chase

I hope that readers have not turned the pages of this chapter quickly to get to my analysis of the Grand National, because I am afraid that I have no positive advice. Even though the fences have become easier and the going is rarely as heavy as it used to be, I consider this a race to avoid. The difficulty is not the possibility that your selection will be brought down, or be badly hampered in running through a large field of moderate horses. It is that there are no useful form/statistics patterns.

The statistical trends (over 9 years, because of the void race in 1993) are:

Age: 5/9 winners were aged 10 and over

In other races, this would be a useful statistic, since not many big handicaps are won by older horses. However, in the last 9 runnings of this race, 204 of the runners were aged 10 years+, as opposed to 117 aged 9 and younger, so the result is not surprising.

Weight: 9/9 carried 10st 8lbs or less

Rating: 9/9 were rated between 142-155

The statistics don't rule in or out many candidates, and the difficulties increase immediately you start to sift the candidates on the basis of form. All the 1990s winners were running over the National fences for the first time; and only two of the winners had succeeded over a distance remotely near that of the National (EARTH SUMMIT, 1998, had won over 3m 6f, 6 furlongs shorter; LORD GYLLENE, 1997, had won over 4m 2f, but then was beaten, with no extenuating reason, over the same distance).

My only suggestion for this race, if you must bet, is to focus on the horses in the weight and rating band, read the press comments carefully, and look for a 'possible' horse with some recent form. On the few occasions (2/9) when the going is soft or heavy, look for a horse with a semblance of form on this type of going.

John Hughes Memorial 2m 6f handicap chase

One of those races which, for no obvious reason, does not follow a clear pattern. Thus in the years 1990-2000:

Age: 7 and 8 yos have the best record, but not to the exclusion of other age groups

Rating: 10/10 winners were rated within 10 pounds of Racing Post's top mark

This is quite a tough race, being run over the Grand National course. Very few races are run over this unusual distance, so does it favour speedsters from a shorter distance (around 2m 4f) or stayers (around 3m 1f)? The record shows that 7/10 were in the former category; and to be more precise, 6 of the last 8 had won at 2m 4f earlier in the season.

In most years, this restriction excludes about 1/3rd of the runners. Of these, only one winner (DUBLIN FLYER, 1995) had outstandingly good form credentials, winning at Ascot and Cheltenham respectively. Incidentally, DUBLIN FLYER was trained by the late, lamented Captain T A Forster, an outstanding trainer of staying chasers, a man for whom any race not a handicap chase over less than 3 miles in heavy going was an undignified sprint.

Red Rum 2m handicap chase

Given that the prize money for this race kept pace with inflation throughout the 1990s, to reach £30,000 in 2000, it has always been a race poorly contested by small fields. The trends are:

Age: 9/10 winners are 8 y o or 9 y o

This age group is also significantly over-represented, with the 9 winners coming from 81 runners, whereas the single victory from a different group, an 11 y o, was from 32 runners.

Rating: 7/10 were rated 143+

But there are no more clues, since the race has a rather shady form background. Two of the winners had not won a handicap, not a good sign so late in the season; 1 put back in distance; and four of the handicap winners had won in tiny (3 or 4 runner) fields.

AYR

A fair, galloping track, with testing fences.

Scottish Grand National 4m 1f handicap chase

There are no useful statistical trends.

Age: 5/10 winners were 9 years or older. However, this age group also supplied a disproportionately large number of runners, so this is not a helpful statistic.

Weight: 7/10 carried 11st 0lbs or less

What is surprising is that three winners carried 11st 10lbs (compared to the abysmal record of high weights in the Grand National). The only explanation which I can offer is that there have been some poor quality fields for this race.

Rating: no pattern

The records show that, because of its distance, there is no real pointer to this race. An obvious trial would be the Tote Northern National, a handicap over the same distance run in the middle of February. However, few horses try to win both races. In the 1990s, only one winner of the Tote Northern National (WILLSFORD, 1995) made the attempt; two others - YOUNG KENNY (unseated in the Tote Northern National, last time out) and FOUR TRIX (4th in the Tote Northern National and pulled up in his previous race) - did not make much of a show in that race, but won here.

Only two winners (RUN FOR FREE, 1993; WILLSFORD, 1995) had won over 3m 5f+ in the current season; five had won at a variety of distances from 3m to 3m 4f; and three winners had not won at all during the season. In sum, the lack of statistical trends and form patterns makes this a race to avoid.

CHELTENHAM

The Newmarket of National Hunt racing, or, if you have a particular fondness for National Hunt, the other way round. Oddly enough, there are also two courses here. The Old Course and the New Course are of similar conformation, left-handed and about 12f round, and share a long (about 4 furlongs) and punishing uphill finish.

The highlight of the National Hunt season is the three day Festival meeting, held on the Old Course run near St. Patrick's Day (17 March). The races are all extremely competitive, but of the six handicaps, only two are 'trappy', and in most seasons, there are usually one or two good bets at this meeting. The betting market is, in modern terms, quite staggering, only matched by the Festival meetings at Galway and Listowel. At all the meetings, good form at the other uphill finish courses, Ascot, Haydock, and Sandown, or one of the courses here, is an absolute must. Be sceptical about Kempton and Newbury winners, as Cheltenham is a completely different type of course. Outside the Festival, there are two big handicaps, both run on the New Course, in November and December.

Thomas Pink Gold Cup 2m 4 Ωf chase New Course

This is the first big handicap of the National Hunt season.

Age: aged winners 0/27

Rating: 10/10 rated 134 above

On close examination, the statistical trends do not offer much insight into this race. The form trends exist, but are difficult to interpret. 8 of the 1990s winners had previously won at Cheltenham, and 7 had finished in the first four at t the previous season's Festival. However, 8 had also won or been placed over a longer distance. My evaluation of the race is that it is too early in the season to weigh up previous form and distance preferences, so it should be avoided.

Tripleprint Gold Cup 2m 5f chase New Course

Two races in the 1990s were abandoned (1995 and 1990), leaving only 8 for analysis, which resulted in the following trends:

Age: 8/8 6-9 year olds

Rating: 8/8 134+ in ratings

The only form trend is: to win a good quality 2m 4f handicap (LEGAL RIGHT 1999 Newbury; DUBLIN FLYER 1994 Kempton). The form of the 'obvious' trial for this race, the Thomas Pink Gold Cup, run 4 weeks previously over the same course and half a furlong shorter, does not work out particularly well. Only one winner of that race, SENOR EL BETRUTTI (1997), has tried for the double, and won. In all, 18 horses who made the frame in the earlier race have run here, but only one (ADDINGTON BOY, 1996) has won.

Although it is a month later than the Thomas Pink Gold Cup, in my view there is still not enough current form to enable you to weigh up this race, so it too should be avoided.

There are six big handicaps at the Festival meeting in March.

County 2m1f handicap hurdle Old Course

Age: no pattern

Rating: 10/10 winners were rated 119-135 The statistics offer some guidance, and the form signals are equally mixed.

The Imperial Cup, Sandown is a fair guide to this race, with two winners successful at Cheltenham (1998 BLOWING WIND, Pipe; 1990 MOODY MAN, Hobbs) but three losers (1997 CARLITO BRIGANTE, Webber; 1996 AMANCIO, Harwood; 1994 PRECIOUS BOY, Meagher). Otherwise, the winners in the 1990s included one winner put back in distance (1995); one which had not won that season (1994); and four which had not won a handicap. The handicap winners had won at Carlisle, Kelso, and Warwick. With all due respect to these courses, they are not usually pointers to the biggest N.H. meeting of the season!

Overall, this is a 'neutral' race, in that the form pattern and the statistics sometimes coincide to suggest a selection.

Coral Cup 2m5f handicap hurdle Old Course

This is a new race, which has only been staged for 7 years.

Age: 6/7 were 7 y o +

Rating: 7/7 were rated 144 or less

The form trends are not so clear. M Pipe has won the race twice, once with a winner at Haydock over 2m 4f (BIG STRAND 1997), but also with a winner of the 2m Imperial Cup, Sandown (OLYMPIAN 1993). One of the winners had not won a hurdle handicap (TOP CEES 1998), and another (CHANCE COFFEY 1995) had not won that season, so this is rather a trappy race.

Grand Annual 2m 110yds chase Old Course

This race seemed to favour younger rather than older horses:

Age: 7/10 8 y o or younger

Rating: 7/10 were rated 139 or less

However, the age pattern is not a very definite trend, given the high proportion of runners from age group, so there really is no pattern in the statistics.

Recent form is an advantage, as the most recent five winners had run only four times or fewer during the current season. However, this seems to be a race for horses with little experience in handicaps, as 5/10 had not won a handicap. In the other races, only EDREDON BLEU (1998) had any recent handicap form, having won a 2m handicap at Sandown. All in all, this is definitely a 'trappy' race.

Ladbroke 3m2f handicap hurdle Old Course

Age: no pattern

Rating: 10/10 winners were in the handicap proper

The rating requirement usually means that about half the runners are here to make up the numbers, and without a chance.

This is an unusual distance, and the form requirements are not very clear. 7/10 winners have won over 3m at a flat course, while the Sandown Tote Trophy (2m 6f), although a good four furlongs shorter, has provided two winners from good performances.

Mildmay of Flete 2m 4 Ωf handicap chase Old Course

This is one of the few Cheltenham Festival races of any kind which has two very marked trends:

Age: no pattern

Weight: 9/10 carried 11st 0lbs or less

Rating: 9/10 rated between 129-141

The form guidelines are not quite so definite. Good recent form is essential, as 9/10 winners were first or second within their last two outings. Surprisingly for Cheltenham, some of these winners came from lower class courses (Warwick, Leicester, Hereford).

William Hill 3m1f handicap chase Old Course

There is one apparent trend:

Age: 7/10 winners were aged 9 y o or over

On closer examination, this trend is not significant since relative to the number of runners this age group is not over-represented. 3/39 winners (7.7%) were 7 and 8 y o; 7/87 (8.0%) were 9+.

Weight: no pattern

Rating: no pattern

Nor are there any form guidelines. Five of the winners had at some previous point won at a good class course, but only 2 of these had won recently over the distance. Improving young horses with good recent form seem to have something of a chance, but it isn't possible to be too definite, which makes this race one of the 'neutral' type.

CHEPSTOW

A left handed course almost two miles round, Chepstow has long, undulating straights and sharp bends. On the final run-in of five furlongs, there are five evenly spaced fences. Given these peculiar conditions, a course win is essential. But the form is reliable even at higher class courses.

Sometimes speed figures can be informative about a course, as well as particular horses. An interesting article by (Topspeed) James Willoughby in the Racing Post (27 December 2000) claimed that '...conditions at Chepstow vary more than at any other course. When the going is soft, runners are slowed down to an enormous extent compared to the speeds they can achieve on good to firm.' This suggests that form over the going on this course is also crucial. National Hunt racing at Chepstow is generally of a good standard, much better than on the Flat.

It is a pity that there is only one big handicap at Chepstow, run just after Christmas:

The Welsh National 3m 6f handicap chase Age: 6/7* 9 years or younger
Weight: 6/7 less than 10st 13lbs
Rating: 6/7 137 plus
* the 1995 and 1996 meetings were abandoned; the 1994 run at Newbury
While the statistics don't offer any decisive pointers, this is an outstanding form race. The Rehearsal Chase certainly lives up to its name, as five of the winners here had finished 11215 in the previous race. As a sign of the importance of course form, two of the winners (EDMOND 1999, KENDAL CAVALIER 1998) had been first and second respectively in a 3m 2f race.

DONCASTER

In my view, Doncaster ranks with Haydock as the best of the northern steeplechase courses. The course sets a good test, since it is a good gallop, and the fences are quite stiff. Even when heavy, the going is even across the course, so that it does not lead to false results, if there are going specialists in the field. Unfortunately, the general standard of racing is not quite as high as on the Flat, and there is only one big handicap.

Great Yorkshire Chase 3m handicap chase
Age: 7/8* were 9 or younger
Weight: no trend
Rating: 8/8 were rated 127-142
* abandoned 1992, 1995
A closer analysis of the age trend shows that this is a race for younger hors-

es. 7 and 8 y o s won 5 times from 35 runners (14%), 9 y o s won twice from 38 (5%) and 10 y o s only once from 43 attempts (2.5%).

This is a good race for form trends. 7 out of the 8 winners had won one of their previous 2 starts, and were generally progressive types. However, a word of warning - three of the winners were still at the novice stage, since they had not previously won a handicap.

HAYDOCK

If the public in this part of the world were more enthusiastic about racing, then Haydock might stage even better quality racing. It is a first-class National Hunt course, with a fine galloping circuit and a long run in of almost 5 furlongs. Its big, drop fences are an excellent preparation for Aintree, and they are the second (to Aintree) most testing of any steeplechase course. The racing is generally of a higher standard than the Flat, but the two big handicap chases in January and February (the Peter Marsh over 3m; and the De Vere Gold Cup, formerly the Grand National Trial, over 3m 4 Ωf often attract only weakish fields. Haydock form is top class and can be relied on at all the leading meetings, including the Cheltenham Festival.

De Vere Gold Cup 3m 41/2f chase
Age: 4/9* winners were 10 y o +
Weight: 5/9 carried 10st 8lbs or less
Rating: no trend
* run at Kempton in 1994

The record of aged (10 y o+) horses is not significant in proportion to the number of runners, but it does suggest that this is a rather uncompetitive race. In 2000, the turn-out for this £58,000 prize, a higher prize than for some of the Cheltenham festival races, was a disappointing seven.

There are no form trends, as the winners come from a variety of distances, ranging from 2m 4f to 4m 1f, which makes this race 'trappy'.

Peter Marsh 3m handicap chase
Age: 5/10 winners were 10 years+
Older horses (10 years+) have a good record (5-23), slightly better than 7 and 8 year olds (4-23).
Weight: no pattern
Rating: 8/10 rated 150+

Course and distance winners do well here, having won 4 of the 9 contests (THE LAST FLING 2000; GENERAL WOLFE 1999, 1998; TWIN OAKS 1992). This is usually a competitive race, and as the analysis above shows, it has a clear form/statistics pattern.

The only other handicap worth mentioning, the 2m Swinton handicap hurdle, occurs at an odd point in the season, two weeks after the Whitbread Gold Cup. Seven of the ten winners in the 1990s had not won a handicap, so this is a race to avoid.

KEMPTON

This right-handed track favours course and distance specialists. It is sharp, rather than galloping, so it is not a major test of stamina. The fences do not appear to be very testing, but often floor lazy or indifferent jumpers. Kempton form is often rather puzzling, and best taken with a great deal of salt when you are analysing races at Ascot, Cheltenham, Newbury or Sandown.

The general standard of National Hunt racing here is probably higher than on the Flat, but there is only one really top class handicap, run on the third weekend of February.

Racing Post Chase 3m
Age: 6/10 winners were 10 y o+
Weight: 9/10 winners carried 10st 7lbs+
Rating: 9/10 rated 140+

Surprisingly for a race with such good prize money (£43,500 in 2000), almost half the runners have been aged 10 or more, with a slightly better strike rate than their younger rivals. The statistics suggest that the race tends to be won by an old and experienced campaigner, but is the form record a further help? Course-and-distance winners which have not been put back in distance have won three times (DESERT ORCHID 1990; ZETA'S LAD 1993; and the ill-fated novice, GLORIA VICTIS, 2000); one such winner (DR LEUNT 1999) then won over 3m 2f at Cheltenham before returning here. This race can be difficult to weigh up, as in some years there are no form contenders. It is not an outstanding race for form/statistics, but neither is it trappy when there are form horses, so I put this down as a 'neutral' race.

NEWBURY

It is a great pity that there are only two big handicaps at Newbury, the Hennessy Gold Cup and the Tote Gold Trophy, as it deserves more. Although the course is flat and the fences are no more than averagely testing, it is still a demanding course. In a competitive field, there is always a good gallop round the wide sweeping bends and on the long 5 furlongs run in to the line. Form works out well here, particularly from Ascot, Cheltenham and Sandown. The galloping nature of the course seems to defeat winners from Kempton, which is a sharp course, with tighter bends and shorter straights. However, because it is a flat course, Newbury form does not work out at the uphill finish courses.

Hennessy Gold Cup (3m 2^{1}/2f chase)

Run at the end of November it is the second big handicap chase of the season, and with a first prize of £52,000 well worth making special preparation. By 2000, there were are some well established trends:

Age: 0/34 winners were older than 9
Rating: 10/10 rated 135-162
Weight: 9/10 carried 11st 0lbs or less

The age and ratings pattern is a reasonable pointer. For example, in 2000 it excluded half of the 18 runners, although admittedly only one of these had otherwise much of a chance on form.

The form required for this race is a win at a good class or middle rank course, such as Chepstow, Haydock (the Edward Hanmer Chase - 2/3 winners), Newbury or Wincanton (the Badger Beer Chase). Penalised runners have a reasonable record, with 4 winners (TEETON MILL, 1998; SUNY BAY 1997; COOME HILL 1996; and COULDN'T BE BETTER 1995).

Tote Gold Trophy (2m1/2f hurdle)

This valuable race (£58,000 in 2001)appears at a good point in the season, just over a month before Cheltenham, so that many of the runners will already have shown some form. There are usually very few seasonal debutants in the race.

Age: 8/9* winners aged 7 or less
Rating: 9/9* winners rated 132-147

* race abandoned in 1991

The statistical pattern is reasonably helpful. Similarly the form pattern, which shows that a recent victory over the distance or over 2m 1f at Ascot, Cheltenham or Sandown is an invaluable pointer.

NEWCASTLE

A left-handed galloping course, with stiff fences. This is a highly demanding course, an excellent test, particularly when the going is soft.

Tote Northern National 4m 1f chase

Formerly the Eider Chase, this race is run in the third week of February.

Age: 5/8* winners were 9 y o or younger, but proportionate to the number of runners, no age group has an advantage

Weight: 6/8* winners carried 10st 6lbs or less Rating: 5/8 were rated 128 or less

* race abandoned 1991 and 1994

The only form clue is that 6/8 winners had won over 3m 4f+ this season.

However the record is balanced by the fact that only 3 of these 9 winners (to 2000) were trained by top flight or middle ranking trainers.

SANDOWN

Sandown is a top class jumping course, with tough fences and a draining uphill finish. It is a specialists' course, since in the back straight there are three fences (the 'railway fences') within 200 yards, which usually defeat inexperienced runners.

While the quality of Flat racing has declined in the last decade, the National Hunt programme has flourished. There are four big handicaps, and usually some good quality supporting races.

Imperial Cup 2m1/2f handicap hurdle

Age: 9/10 7 year old or younger

Rating: 7/10 rated 125 or less

The statistics point to a young, lowly-rated horse as the winner of this race, but as this type usually makes up three-quarters of the field, does the form pattern help to focus on the likely victor? Apparently not, as 6 of the winners had no recent form, and the other 4 had won a novice hurdle at Wetherby, and handicaps at Ayr, Fontwell and Stratford.

Although this is a trappy race, it is a useful pointer to the Cheltenham Festival. Two winners went on to win the County Hurdle at Cheltenham (1998 BLOWING WIND, Pipe; 1990 MOODY MAN, Hobbs) and three lost (1997 CARLITO BRIGANTE, Webber; 1996 AMANCIO, Harwood; 1994 PRECIOUS BOY, Meagher). One winner, OLYMPIAN (1993), won the 2m 5f Coral Cup at Cheltenham.

Tote 2m 6f handicap hurdle

Age: no pattern, except that 0/10 aged runners won

Rating: no more than 140

The statistics are moderately informative, but there are some useful form patterns. Only one of the winners was being put back in distance (from 3m), while 8 had won races from 2m 4f - 2m 6f. Form shown at a good class course, preferably with an uphill finish, is a useful pointer, as 7 of the winners had this profile. This is a mid-level prize (£29,000 in 2001), and the leading trainers sometimes give it a miss. It is a key race for the Cheltenham Festival if you are willing to take a chance on distances, with RUBHANUNISH (2000) and MIRACLE MAN (1995) winning over 3m 2f, and TRAINGLOT (1996) over 2m 5f.

Whitbread Gold Cup 3m 5f handicap chase

The middle rank trainers seem to have a better record than the leading stables, which are perhaps unwilling to risk their horses in what is the final big handicap (run at the end of April) in the British winter season.

At first sight, there are two trends (to 1999):

Weight: 8/10 carried no more than 10st 5lbs

Age: 0/14 were 7 year olds

Younger horses (aged 6) rarely run in this race, and 9/10 year olds have won a respectable 6/71 strike rate.

The statistics usually suggest the elimination of about one-third of the runners. But a closer look at the form is less reassuring. Only one of the winners had form at a comparable distance, and all the others were either put back in distance or had won at 3m - 3m 2f. This is rather a tricky race, as the trends demonstrate, probably due to its unusual distance and its position in the season.

William Hill 2m 110y handicap hurdle

The first major handicap hurdle in the NH season, this race does not show any statistical trends.

It is usually (7/10) won by one of the leading trainers, with Pipe winning the race four times. Despite all these positive indicators, this is sometimes a difficult race to predict, since 6 of the winners did not have suitable recent form. Of these, 3 had not won a handicap, and 3 had not won this season. The winners with good recent form, and the right trend characteristics, were justifiably made short-priced favourites, so the race, though not one to be avoided, is 'neutral', and not one of my favourites.

UTTOXETER

An 11f round, left-handed course, undulating with rather tight bends, and a fair, but not testing course. It has always been regarded as one of the best second rank courses, but under the canny direction of Stan Clarke, it may yet move up a grade. Uttoxeter stages two big handicaps: the National Trial (beginning of February, worth £37,700 in 2001) and the Midlands Grand National (first Saturday after the Cheltenham March meeting, £43500 in 2000).

It is only quite recently that the former has attracted substantial prize money, so it is too early to form an opinion about form/statistics trends.

Midlands Grand National 4m 2f handicap chase

Before 1992, the race was run over 4m, so there is only 7 years worth of form at the current distance.

Age: 03/08 10 y o +
Weight: 05/08 won off 10st 3lbs or less
Rating: 06/08 rated 130 or below

The statistics suggest that a light weight, rather lowly rated horse has a better than average chance. In terms of form, the obvious preparation is the 4m 1f Tote Northern National (formerly Eider Chase), run about 6 weeks previously at Newcastle. Since 1993, 2 winners have tried, with one loser and one winner (SEVEN TOWERS 1997). Other winners had form over 3m 4f+, but the record is patchy, as two of the winners had not scored at during the season. In sum, this is a 'neutral' race, meaning that it is neither trappy nor a clear form/statistics event.

Irish Racing

I must apologise to the reader for the slightly uneven treatment of National Hunt racing in Ireland, particularly in relation to the winter season. It is only in the last two years or so that coverage of Irish racing in the press and the form books has reached the same level of detail which British racing fans have taken for granted for many years.

FAIRYHOUSE

A right handed course, just over 14f round, with a run in of almost 3 furlongs, and a slight uphill finish.

The Festival meeting at Easter has some good racing, and one big handicap.

Irish Grand National 3m 5f handicap chase

Age: no trend
Weight: no trend
Rating: no trend

There are no statistical trends, and, for such a valuable race (£78,000 in 2000), the form is just as mystifying. Some rather average horses have won this race, and recent form seems completely at a discount. If you had to clutch at straws, then grasp at any form over 3m or thereabouts shown much earlier in the season, even if this means ignoring several poor performances. Perhaps, like the Whitbread Gold Cup, this race comes at an odd moment in the season as far as predictability is concerned. A race to avoid.

GALWAY

Right-handed and only 7f round, with an uphill run to the last fence, Galway might seem to be the Irish steeplechase equivalent to Chester. The course is not idyllic as it sounds, set in an industrial estate and a strong competitor for Wolverhampton in the glamour stakes. But it is fairly stamina-testing, since the long downhill run to the final two fences precedes a stiff climb to the finish.

At the Festival meeting (end of July), the prize money leaps ahead every year, and the betting market is awash with cash, getting stronger as the Celtic Tiger awakes. Galway is the highpoint of the summer season, and every Irish trainer wants to win the big races here.

Galway Plate 2m 6f handicap chase

Always the most prestigious race at this meeting, in the year 2000 the prize money was increased by 50% to £61,250. Age: no trend; winners come from all ages, as young as 5 and as old as 10. Rating: no trend

The statistics are unrevealing, but the form pattern is more encouraging. In the last 8 occurrences to 1999, four of the winners had either not won a handicap or were put back in distance; in the other four, the winners had shown recent form over the distance.

In summary, the race can be won by a horse with good form or a course and distance winner (MOSCOW EXPRESS 1999; LIFE OF A LORD 1996, 1995; FEATHERED GALE 1994), but in other years if there is no such qualifier, the race is usually won by horses with no form at all.

LEOPARDSTOWN

A left-handed course, 14f round, and a testing uphill finish of just under 3 furlongs.

Leopardstown stages good class racing throughout the winter season, with the main meeting taking place in the three days after Christmas. The most valuable race is the 3m Paddy Power.com Handicap Chase, worth £71,250 in 2000. However, since the race has only been so richly endowed since 1996, it is too early to decide whether there any form/statistics patterns. The first signs are not encouraging, as none of the five winners had any good recent form. Typically, for instance, the most recent victory of the 2000 winner, CALL ME DARA, was a modest handicap at Thurles, 11 months previously.

LISTOWEL

A flat, rectangular, left-handed course, only 8f round.

The Festival meeting, in the third week of September, second only to Galway in popularity and the strength of the betting market. Like all west of Ireland courses, the going can change very quickly even in September, so always make sure you have up-to-date information. The racing programme is not quite as strong as at Galway, but there is one big handicap.

Kerry Grand National Chase 3m handicap

The prize money for this race has begun to catch up with the pretensions of its title, as it rose by 78% (in money terms) during the four years to 2000.

Age: no trend
Weight: no trend
Rating: no trend

A difficult race to sum up. The winners come from the entire range of the handicap. DEEP BRAMBLE (1993) DORANS PRIDE (1997) and LIFE OF A LORD (1995) all carried 11st 6 lbs or more, while the others came from lower in the handicap. Older horses (10 y o upwards) are slightly under-represented among the winners (two in the last decade), but this is not a significant trend.

Nor is the form record any clearer. Although the courses are as dissimilar as they could be, since Galway is right-handed, with an uphill finish, the winners of the Galway Plate (2m 6f) or the 2m 6f handicap at the Galway September meeting are often aimed at this race. In the last decade, 8 runners have tried to follow this route. Discounting HEIST (1997) because he had only won a 4 runner race last time out, the bare result is not decisive, with a tally of two winners.

PUNCHESTOWN

A right-handed course, undulating, and about 2m round. A wide, galloping course, at which form works out quite well.

The Punchestown Festival at the end of April / beginning of May is the best of the meetings. There are 3 handicap chases (over 2m, 3m1f, and 3m 2f) and 3 handicap hurdles (over 2m, 2m 2f, and 2m 4f) at this meeting, which marks the end of the National Hunt winter/spring season. Although the courses are quite different, the Fairyhouse meeting, about a fortnight earlier, and the Cheltenham Festival, six weeks earlier, are a good preparation. More demanding than Aintree, it is not as gruelling as Cheltenham when the going is soft. Although one or two English trainers have realised that the Punchestown meeting is a highly entertaining place to be, their interest is not matched by the results, as the meeting tends to be dominated by the local trainers. Some Irish trainers who send few or unsuccessful runners to England, do well at this meeting (e.g. A L T Moore, W P Mullins).

★★★
NATIONAL HUNT TRAINERS

The names of the star trainers will come as no surprise to even the most casual follower of National Hunt racing:

N Henderson

M C Pipe

N A Twiston-Davies

As on the Flat, there are several trainers perfectly capable of winning big handicaps, but they do so on a less regular basis. With no implication that they are any the less talented, the following trainers can win big handicaps if they have the right material:

A L T Moore (Ireland)

W P Mullins (Ireland)

P F Nicholls

Mrs. Reveley (northern)

N J Henderson

From my point of view, Henderson is the best of the National Hunt trainers. He has an outstanding record in the big handicaps, in which he is a master at placing his runners to best advantage. His methods are predictable, and he rarely has more than two runners per handicap, which makes it easier to weigh up their chances. In particular, he has a very good record at the Cheltenham Festival. His training programme throughout the season is geared to this meeting, and he has relatively few fancied runners in the early part of the season. He is a very patient trainer, and good at bringing a horse back from a long layoff. To round off a perfect picture, he is open with the racing press. To mix the animal metaphors, his swans are swans, so you can trust him when he declares that he has found a good horse.

M C Pipe

What can one say about this brilliant trainer? Nothing at all original, except to say that anyone who spends as much time analysing a winner's performance as a loser's deserves all the success he has gained. Not from a conventional training background, it is well known that he has revolutionised National Hunt training methods. Not only does he hoover up the prizes at the lesser tracks, but his record in big handicaps is just as impressive. However much he has questioned the conventional ways of training, in placing his horses for big handicaps, Pipe generally does the obvious, with great effect.

I say 'generally', because sometimes his runners make great leaps forward in distance or are put back in distance, and still win. This disregard for distance is not peculiar to Pipe, but is a feature of National Hunt racing which anyone who swears by the form book just has to accept. You also have to follow the form book quite carefully when looking at Pipe's runners in the big handicaps. He often has three or more runners in the same race, and you must learn to ignore those which are running out of their class. Finally, there is one odd feature about Pipe's record. More than any other leading trainer I can think of, his stable goes through relatively bad patches for a month or two. However, these are usually periods when there are fairly few big handicaps, so they do not affect his record in this type of race.

N A Twiston-Davies

Twiston-Davies is as likely to be informative about his horse's chances as an MI6 officer is to publish a list of his agents. He has very much come to rival Pipe in the art of preparing a horse for the big race, but his methods are far less obvious.

But there is no doubt that he is very gifted, with an outstanding record in the big handicaps. His horses tend to be rather tough, and able to stand up to hard racing once they hit form, such as RUBHANISH (1999).

Chapter 5: Betting in the big handicaps

This is the shortest, but the most useful chapter in the whole book. I have met far more backers who make inspired selections than those who are equally clever about backing their selections. Most backers pay far more attention to making a selection than to their betting strategy. Even with a strike rate which in percentage terms seems too low to enable you to come out on on top (25-30%), you can still make your betting pay if you have a considered approach.

Betting strategy in big handicaps is exactly the same as in any other kind of handicap. The main difference is that if you look for value along the lines suggested later in this chapter, you will find more, not fewer, opportunities for a good bet in the big handicaps. First of all, to the basics. Most backers could improve the returns on their outlay by adopting five simple rules: think long-term; keep a record of your bets; only bet to win; never bet at short prices; and adopt a simple staking plan.

Think long-term. Most punters think of making a profit on the day, or even during the meeting, whereas you should look at your betting in the perspective of a season. Even if you bet much more frequently at the big meetings than my approach would suggest, or if you also bet on non-handicaps, then I doubt if you can find more than three or four bets per meeting. If you are careful about making your selection, then maybe a month to six weeks will pass by until a good chance comes up to turn the selection into a bet.

The bookmakers have to bet in every race; if you have the patience, you can wait until the odds are in your favour.

Keep a record of your bets. How many of the phoneline 'services'/tipsters/ systems sellers who make such enticing claims in the sporting press or over the Internet either publish a complete record of their selections, or will supply you with such a record upon application?

Apply the same principle to your own betting, to see where your money is going. For this purpose, you need to keep a record of every bet you make. Keep your betting slips, and analyse your own pattern of betting. You will soon be able to distinguish between the 'silly' bets, where you had a bet for no very good reason at all, and your carefully considered selections. Of course, it is always possible that your 'silly' bets are much more successful, in which case throw away the form books and read no further!

Only bet to win. In certain types of race, it may be worth betting each way or even place only (on the Tote), but in big handicaps I prefer to bet win only. My records show that my losing selections tend to run down the field rather than be placed, in which case an each way bet is even more money lost. This result shows the value of keeping records : if your losing selections frequently run into a place, then the place element of an each-way bet is a useful saver. Most backers are wary of supporting more than one horse in a race, perhaps because they are loth to admit that they may have backed more than one loser in a race! But if you cannot decide between two selections, if the odds about both are long enough, it can often be worth while to split your bet.

Never bet at short prices. How short is short, in a big handicap? Punters seem to be peculiarly fascinated by odds-on shots, as if their short price represented a weight of inspired money: this is a bandwagon which they have to climb on. Fortunately, odds-on chances hardly ever occur in the big handicaps, so the temptation to throw yourself beneath the wheels of the odds-on juggernaut rarely arises.

If you follow a systematic approach to making your selections, then it is easy to assess a short price. Every selection then has as good a chance as every other selection, so that in your opinion every selection has a 100% chance. If you reject a particular horse, then you consider that it has a 0% chance. In my book, there is no such thing as, say, a 50% chance: a runner either has a 0% or a 100% chance. Adopting this method of selection greatly simplifies your betting strategy. You don't have to think: what odds should I accept about a 30% or a 70% chance? All you need to think about is the relationship between price and strike rate, as follows. Assuming an average strike rate of 30% (3 winners in 10 bets), then you can see where the break even point lies.

STRIKE RATE	ODDS	RETURN ON £100 (10 bets of £10)
30%	2-1 -	-£10
30%	5-2	+£05
30%	3-1	+£20
30%	7-2	+£35
30%	4-1	+£50

The break even point is somewhere between 9-4 and 5-2. If you pay the higher rate of tax on your bets, then it is nearer 3-1. I think that, to allow for a margin of error, 7-2+ is the safest betting level.

Look at the matter the other way round. In order to break even, what strike rate is necessary at a given starting price?

STARTING PRICE	STRIKE RATE
6-4	40%
2-1	33%
5-2	29%
3-1	25%
7-2	22%
4-1	20%

Notice that as the prices lengthen, the returns increase, and the break-even strike rate falls. If you have the nerve to do so, it makes sense to bet more at long prices. This does take a lot of self-confidence, because it seems that if a runner is at a long price, or if its price lengthens, then there must be something 'wrong' with it today. But if you keep a cool head and make a clear distinction between your estimate of its chance, and, the price offered, then it is logical to bet more, not less, on long priced runners. Look at this way. You want to buy a shirt at the sales. Before you go to the shop, you have a clear idea of what you want, and you are prepared to pay, say, £20. In the shop you see a shirt which looks just right, and is offered at £10. What do you do? I guess that many people would think, where's the catch? there must be something wrong with it which isn't obvious, so I won't buy one. It would be more logical, but counter-intuitive, to buy 2 or even 4 shirts at this price.

Of course this does not mean that you should bet more or even consider it as a selection just because it is at a long price. This is what punters call, mistakenly in my view, 'looking for value.' They weigh up a race by comparing the odds on offer with their 'percentage' view of the chances, as follows:

PERCENTAGE CHANCE ODDS OFFERED
Runner A 80%   **2-1**
Runner B 50%   **3-1**
Runner C 40%   **6-1**
Runner D 30%   **5-1**

The 'looking for value' commentary goes something like this: 'Runner A has an obvious chance and is no value as 2-1 favourite. The value bet in this race is Runner C, as he has a good chance and is an outstanding 6-1 etc.' In my view, Runner C is simply not a bet at any price. This 'looking for value' approach puts matters back to front: it looks at the price, and asks, does it have a chance, whereas you should ask exactly the opposite question: it has a chance, does it have a price? So the trick is only to bet when you think that your selection has a fixed chance, and then assess the starting price in relation to your strike rate.

Adopt a simple staking plan. The aim of any staking plan should be to help you cut your losses and capitalise on your winnings. 'Cutting your losses' is the more difficult, as when you are on a losing streak, it is tempting to think that one or big bets will set matters right. It is like putting your foot down on the accelerator when you are running down hill out of control.

You have to have a system which you have settled on before your losing streak, as it is usually difficult to think clearly and rationally during the losing runs which afflict every backer, even the most successful professionals.

The simplest system, which is purely mechanical and does not require any judgement for its application, is to set aside a bank of 100 points, and bet 10% of your bank on every bet. You add your winnings to the bank, and subtract the losses. The main point of the system is psychological, not mathematical. In fact, for some sequences of bets, the 10% system gives much poorer results than a level staking system. But in the sequences which involve long losing runs, it puts the brakes on when you are in a downhill period.

There is one, slightly riskier variant of the 10% system which is worth considering. It depends on the idea that you should bet more, not less, at longer prices.

PRICE	PROPORTION OF THE BANK
7-2	10.0%
4-1	12.5%
9-2	15.0%
5-1	17.5%
11-2+	20.0%

It is riskier because if a series of 11-2+ prices occur during a downhill spiral then they are the accelerator, not the brake, which you need during these periods. But this is quite unlikely, as there is no connection between the kind of prices you are likely to be offered, and, the sequence of winners and losers. Following these simple rules will save you a great deal of trouble. They can be applied quite mechanically, without any thought. What is more difficult, is to understand what is meant by 'looking for value', one of the biggest cliches in racing. In my view, it means looking for false-priced favourites.

This recommendation is not the same as betting against the favourite, although there is a great deal to be said for doing so. Although I have only checked the results for Newmarket, where all handicaps come into our reckoning, I suspect that they are roughly similar at other courses:

Newmarket (Rowley) 3 yo favourites 15.2%
Newmarket (Rowley) all-aged favourites 19.2%

Using the tables above, this means that in 3 y o races, any Newmarket (Rowley) favourite is a false price if its starting price is less than 11-2, and in all-aged races, if less than 4-1. In both cases, the favourites are below the 'break-even' point and represent poor value.

But my idea of a false-priced favourite does not refer to the relation between the price and the winning ratio for the category of race, but to certain well-established form patterns. If you know that a favourite following these patterns has only a 5-10% chance of winning, then you make a double hit: the favourite's price is short, given its real chance; and, conversely, the prices of some of the other runners are long.

False-priced favourites occur in all kinds of races, including non-handicaps. But according to my records, a higher proportion of favourites are at a false price in the big handicaps than in any other kind of race; and the proportion of losers among these false-priced favourites is also higher than in ordinary handicaps.

In any given race, FPFs cannot always be anticipated. You can usually make a fair guess about the likely FPFs, as the starting-prices in the press are a very good guide. Quite frequently, however, a really unexpected FPF emerges in the betting market a few minutes before the 'off'. Do not be swayed by these last-minute market moves into ignoring the usual rules for identifying an FPF. Over the years I have found that the most surprising FPFs occur in the very strong betting markets at the Irish festival meetings.

It is equally surprising, and quite inexplicable, to find that there is a better strike rate for selections in races where there is a FPF. There is no good reason at all for this discrepancy, as selections are made quite independently of starting price. False-priced favourites can easily be identified, by following a simple series of rules given below, and no judgement has to be exercised. If you would prefer a more intuitive approach, always listen to Barry Dennis's 'Bismarcks' slot on the Morning Line (Channel 4, Saturdays). He has a fantastic strike rate (over 90%) in picking losers, many of which are running in the big handicap. As a bookmaker he is in a much better position than the average punter to make money out of this curious ability, by laying against his 'Bismarcks'. But if there is a Bismarck running in a race for which you have a selection, then you have found a ready-made false-priced favourite. It is helpful to understand why FPFs arise with such frequency. I believe that there are two reasons. The first is the pressure upon journalists to think up an interesting 'story line'. For example, if A appears to run well and almost beat B, when the two horses run again, with the weights now apparently in favour of A, which story line would you prefer as an editor: 'B had the measure of A, and will win again' or 'unlucky A can beat B at the revised weights'?

The second is that for many punters looking for patterns and following rules is too much like everyday life. In their leisure time pursuits people like to find 'the exception that breaks the rule' or the clever rather than the obvious bet.

To avoid an irritating repetition, I will from now on call this type of favourite an FPF. They fall into the following categories, which for ease of reference I will list and deal with in alphabetical order.

ALL WEATHER FORM
COUNTER-TREND
HELD OFF THIS MARK
NOT WON THIS SEASON
NOT WON A HANDICAP
PUT BACK IN DISTANCE

REVERSING THE FORM
UNRELIABLE JUMPER

All Weather Form

While some horses do perform well on both turf and sand, the form shown on the traditional surface has no bearing whatsoever on the outcome of All-Weather racing. An All-Weather favourite on the basis of turf form is a highly reliable type of loser. The best book on All-Weather racing, David Bellingham, Gold from the Sand (Raceform 2000) has a number of examples which prove the point.

So the cardinal rule for eliminating runners is: never (and this is a real, not a politician's, never) back a horse which has not won on the All-Weather. Such non-winners are a great source of false-priced favourites. The journalistic catch-phrases to look for are: 'X's action suggests that he will go well on the All-Weather'; 'Has won on soft going, and should be suited by the All-Weather'. These suggestions are always plausible but rarely fulfilled.

Counter-trend

As you will have noticed, some big handicaps do follow a definite statistical trend, in terms of either age, rating or weight. A runner which goes against this trend is a FPF, even if it would not be discounted on grounds of form.

For instance, the Chester Cup has one marked trend. In the 1990s, 9/10 winners were rated 88 or below. RAINBOW HIGH, rated at 113, was counter to this trend, and an FPF at 9-2.

Held off this mark

It is easy to identify a runner as belonging to the other FPF types, but this one takes a little searching out. If a horse could not win his last race at or even below his present handicap mark, then, given suitable conditions (course, distance, going), there is every reason to suppose that he will find one too good for him in today's race. For the time being, he has reached his level and cannot go any further.

A good example was NATIVE CHARM, in the Mildmay of Flete handicap chase (Cheltenham, 15 March 2000). The Racing Post summary read: '...winning run came to an end at Sandown but was up against...((two)) much-improved ((horses))...remains on handy mark (raised 1 pound) and expected to make her presence felt again.' Even if her mark had not been raised at all, I still would have felt that her winning run had come to an end, and that she did not deserve to be favourite. An even more plausible type, is a runner which runs off the same mark as when losing last time out, and which, by an anomaly in the handicap system, is due to run off a higher mark after today's race.

It might seem that he can take advantage of the anomaly, but this happens so rarely that he still falls within the 'held off this mark' category of FPF.

Not won a handicap

This type occurs in both Flat and National Hunt racing.

At the level of handicap racing we are concerned with, it usually arises when a horse has run well without winning in a Listed race. Such horses then seem a class above handicap races, but their pretensions are usually quickly deflated by other handicappers.

There are one or two exceptions. In the Britannia and the Ebor handicaps non-handicap winners have quite a good record, so that they are not false-priced favourites. Apart from these races, the public seems to have a particular tendency to make some trainers' non-handicap winners a source of favourites, for example Henry Cecil or Sir Michael Stoute. They can, and do, make the abrupt transition from non-handicaps at their first attempt, but they do not have a favourites' chance to do so. They do make a very good story, especially if they have won 'impressively', 'unchallenged', 'in commanding style'.

Even in a big handicap at the Cheltenham Festival, it is possible to find FPFs of this type. In the Ladbroke handicap (14 March 2000) DARAPOUR seemed to have everything in his favour - clever trainer (A P O'Brien), top jockey (C F Swan) and shrewd gambling owner (J P McManus) - except that he had not won a handicap. It is true that he had run well in non-handicaps, but even the magic phrase 'looks to have been laid out for this' could not conceal the fact that he had yet to win a handicap. Hardly the form to justify being made favourite, even at 4-1, in a 24 runner handicap.

Not won a handicap chase

'In the hands of his astute trainer, can be expected to make the transition from the smaller obstacles' is the kind of comment which you should look for. I don't think that even the best trainers can prepare a runner which has only won over hurdles to succeed in a big handicap chase. Schooling a horse at home on his own over a few fences is quite different from setting him to run over at least 16 fences in a competitive field of a dozen or more runners.

Put back in distance

In Flat racing, a horse which is put back in distance, even by a few hundred yards, compared to his most recent win is always an FPF. This type of FPF often occurs when a horse which has won over an easy course, is then put back a furlong in distance, but over an uphill finish - e.g. 'won over 6f at York, will be suited by the stiff 5f at Sandown.'

The rule has to be a little more elastic in N.H. racing. Horses are able to win over a much greater range of distances, but there is a limit: when they are put back more than a furlong compared to their most recent success. This change of distance is much more difficult than being put forward in distance, and makes the runner a definite FPF.

Reversing the Form

This is the best type of false-priced favourite, as it has the highest losing strike rate.

There are two slightly different types.

In a 12f handicap, A beats B by two lengths, and is raised 2 pounds by the official handicapper, while leaving B's mark unchanged. If they meet again over the same distance and under roughly similar conditions, journalists usually comment: 'B can beat A at the revised weights.'

In the second type, A beats B by two lengths, but this time the handicapper raises A's mark by 4 pounds and reduces B's by 1 pound. This time, when they meet again, the newspaper comment is: 'B can take advantage of the pull in the weights to reverse the form.'

For both types, the newspaper comments seem quite plausible. Yet according to my records, B has only a one in twenty chance of turning the tables on A, even if B ran well in defeat or seemed unlucky to lose. It was discovering this pattern which suggested to me that weight is not so important in handicap racing as is usually supposed. The only other explanation which occurs to me is the psychological one: that the jockey riding B may feel at a disadvantage given that B was beaten last time, and he may not feel very confident about the re-match.

Whatever the explanation, the record is clear. So why is it always ignored by the racing press? It is probably because the story line 'A has a 95% chance of beating B again' makes horse-racing seem a rather predictable business, whereas it is much more exciting to read: 'B was an unlucky loser last time out, and is now favoured by the weights' or 'B ran on very well, just failing to catch A, and he should be able to reverse the form'. Even the best trainers are not exempt from this trend. John Gosden's STRAHAN almost beat RAYYAAN in a 7f race at Newmarket. Next time out (05 May 2000), it seemed highly plausible that he would be able to reverse the form, and was made favourite on this basis. The previous form was confirmed exactly, as RAYYAAN won again by a short head.

Unreliable jumper

Be fairly cautious about this type of FPF. You should consider the full spectrum of not quite foot perfect jumpers, descending from the unquestionable

- 'mistakes' / 'hit fence X' - down to and including 'not fluent' / 'pecked on landing'. Your reservation should relate to courses and trainers. It is wisest to restrict this type of FPF to the handicaps at the toughest courses, such as Cheltenham or Sandown. A chancy jumper can sometimes get away with 'fiddling' ('fluking' in racingspeak) his fences at the less demanding courses. An example which comes readily to mind is MOSCOW EXPRESS, winner of the 1999 Galway Plate. Although the top class trainers are capable of correcting a horse's jumping very quickly, it is always wise to wait for the improvement to show itself on the racecourse. At home, a horse may seem to be making dramatic progress, but usually he is only pitted against two or three other horses. On the racecourse, in big handicaps, several other horses are coming at you all the time - it is a completely different experience.

An outstanding example of an FPF of this kind was EXIT SWINGER in the Tripleprint Gold Cup (09 December 2000). In his previous race, at Sandown, when he was second, he had not jumped well, blundering more than once. Sandown is a difficult course, but Cheltenham is even more testing. I thought that the Racing Post comment, 'comparative inexperience over fences is a minor quibble', was misguided, even though EXIT SWINGER was trained by Pipe. He certainly did not justify a price of 7-4 in a valuable 12 runner handicap.

Chapter 6: A Year at the Races

The races are analysed from 2000-2001, so that when reading this chapter, you will see the handicaps as I saw them at the time, i.e. the trend information available to me for the previous ten years.

This chapter will analyse all the big handicaps for one year. It begins with the Cheltenham meeting on 14 March 2000, and concludes with the Imperial Cup, at Sandown, on 10 March 2001. The choice of dates is not significant, as it was determined by the author's deadline.

The 'year' chosen was slightly atypical, in that the final two months of the Flat season were the wettest since about 1750, well before records of racing were kept. A wet season is good for National Hunt racing, as a far higher proportion of horses are capable of acting on soft going. So of course (damp) Sod's Law operated, and the going at Cheltenham was unseasonably firm. Whether or not it was a coincidence, no good sprint handicappers appeared during this year, costing me one or two bets.

Abbreviations

FPF = false-priced favourite
h.o.t.m. = held off this mark
l.t.o. = last time out
NWG = not won on the going
NWTS   = not won this season
PBD = put back in distance

14 March 2000 CHELTENHAM Old Course William Hill 3m1f handicap chase Going: good

There are no significant statistical trends in this race, but on form young improving chasers seem to have a chance. There were two such runners in this race, both winners over 3m and in the care of leading trainers, BEAU (7-10-2, N A Twiston-Davies) and MARLBOROUGH (8-10-3, N J Henderson). I ruled out MARLBOROUGH because he still tended to make too many mistakes. BEAU had the edge in the ratings (-8 as against -11) and had won a good handicap chase, the 3m Great Yorkshire Chase, Doncaster, at the end of January. Last time out he had won a small stakes race at Ascot and, in my viewing of the race, jumped quite well. The very strong betting market at the Festival often produces rather surprising FPFs, which the betting forecast in the Racing Post has not anticipated. SPENDID, at 8-1 well out in the forecast, was 5-1 joint favourite with BEAU, but had not won a handicap chase. The race did produce a form result, but unfortunately not the one I wished for. MARLBOROUGH ran on strongly to beat BEAU quite comfortably by $2^1/2$ lengths.

14 March 2000 CHELTENHAM Old Course
Ladbroke 3m 2f handicap hurdle
Going: good

The only statistical trend, that all the last ten winners had been in the handicap proper, suggested the elimination of 11 of the 24 runners, including Pipe's TAKE CONTROL. Although he had only won a 2m 7 Ωf handicap hurdle at Plumpton, Pipe's runners at Cheltenham are always to be checked very carefully. If he had not been ruled out by the trends, he would have been rather a dark horse.

Of the remaining 13 runners, the only one with sound recent form at a good class course was RUBHAHUNISH, winner of the Tote Handicap at Sandown. He had been driven out to win, but he had jumped cleanly and was a strong horse. When I saw that he was trained by N Twiston-Davies, everything fell into place.

This race shows the difference between my approach and that of Craig Thake's Ten Year Trends in Racing Post. On his very thoroughgoing analysis, DARA-POUR seemed to be in line with the main trends. But he had not won a handicap hurdle, so why was he made 4-1 favourite? The Racing Post commentary suggested that he 'looks to have been laid out for this', so seeing that he was trained by Aidan O'Brien and owned by J P McManus, many punters must have rushed to conclusions.

RUBHAHUNISH ran on strongly up the hill to beat TAKE CONTROL and DARAPOUR quite easily.

15 March 2000 CHELTENHAM Old Course Coral Cup 2m5f
handicap hurdle
Going: good to firm

My analysis of previous years suggested that, perhaps because of the distance, this is a 'trappy' race. Certainly none of the leading trainers had an outstanding form runner, so I decided to leave it alone. The winner, WHAT'S UP BOYS had not won a handicap.

15 March 2000 CHELTENHAM Old Course Mildmay of Flete 2m
$4^1/2$f handicap chase
Going: good to firm

This is one of Cheltenham's races which falls into a reassuringly neat pattern. It has already been analysed in detail in chapter 1, as an example of how to weigh up a handicap.

The limits of the ratings suggested the elimination of 12 of the 20 runners. Of the remaining 8, only the following had good recent form:

D winners (2m^1/2f+)

DARK STRANGER	04 February	Leicester	2m 4f
NATIVE CHARM	15 January	Ascot	h.o.t.m.
INN AT THE TOP	04 March	Doncaster	2m 3f
SIR DANTE	22 January	Kempton	2m 4f

Looking at my handicap ratings:
+2 INN AT THE TOP
-3 SIR DANTE
-4 DARK STRANGER

INN AT THE TOP and SIR DANTE had only won on flat courses, so DARK STRANGER looked a possibility, having won at Leicester, a course with a stiff uphill finish. However, I decided that the form was not of high enough class for the Cheltenham Festival meeting.

The result:
1 DARK STRANGER
2 NATIVE CHARM
3 INN AT THE TOP
4 SIR DANTE

would have been predicted by Eric Morecambe - all the right horses...but not necessarily in the right order!

16 March 2000 CHELTENHAM Old Course Grand Annual 2m 110yds handicap chase

Going: good to firm

The only horse with any recent form was SAMAKAAN. He did fit into the pattern of this race in that respect, but also in that he had not won a handicap chase. For that reason he was an FPF in my view. Nor had his trainer, Venetia Williams, yet proved that she could win this kind of race with a novice. He did win, as a favourite, leaving me with rather mixed feelings: confirming one trend, and confounding another.

16 March 2000 CHELTENHAM Old Course County 2m 1f handicap hurdle

Going: good to firm

For this race, you must look for a horse aged 7 or younger, and rated 119-135, with good form, ideally from the Imperial Cup, Sandown.

Today there was no Imperial Cup winner, and only one runner with good form. Two races ago, MASTER TERN had won over the course and distance, and then won over 2m 2f at Kelso. As a 5 year old rated 130, he was in line with the guiding trends. He was just within my limits for N.H. races, by being put back in distance by a furlong. My only reservation concerned his trainer, J J O'Neill, whom I knew to be very capable, but so far unproven at the very highest level. No bet, but one to monitor. After MASTER TERN had won at 9-2, I began to wonder whether Kelso casts a magic spell on handicap hurdlers. A beautiful course, but even the Duke of Roxburghe would not insist that all its races were top class, so why had three winners of this race in the last decade won previously at Kelso? Evidently O'Neill is on a roll, as in February 2001, the Racing Post reported that he was planning to move southwards, into D Nicholson's old stables. In my view, he is definitely a trainer to follow.

18 March 2000 UTTOXETER Midlands Grand National 4m 2f handicap chase

Going: good

Cheltenham takes a lot of concentration, and before you can have a breather, there is one more National Hunt race before the Flat season begins, and you are in a different world.

Sometimes it must be very frustrating to be a racecourse executive. You hear all the complaints about prize money from owners and trainers, so you offer a decent stake (£43,500) for the Midlands Grand National, and what do you get? A six runner field, of rather average quality.

Only two of the runners, ACKZO and SCOTTON GREEN, seemed to have any chance, respectively in the hands of an up-and-coming (Ferdy Murphy) and established (T D Easterby) trainer. In an exhausting slog through the Newcastle mud in the Tote Northern National, SCOTTON GREEN had beaten ACKZO convincingly. Today the going was good, which did not particularly suit SCOTTON GREEN, but ACKZO seemed to me still rather immature. Both were running off low weights (10st 0lbs), but this seemed to me to be a race to avoid.

SCOTTON GREEN was a tough horse, so I thought he could win again. I could not see ACKZO reversing the form, and was pleased to see that he was a false-priced favourite at 15-8f. Very occasionally such FPFs do win, and this was one of those days, as ACKZO ran on quite well. SCOTTON GREEN was well beaten and reached the limits of his ability for the time being.

25 March 2000 DONCASTER Lincoln 8f handicap

Going: good

The first big handicap of the Flat season is a bookmaker's dream, since only two horses with any form have won in the last 20 years and there are no statistical clues. Some winners have had reasonable All-Weather form, but then so have many losers. The winner, JOHN FERNELEY, had run on well last time out at Wolverhampton. Winners of the Lincoln have a dreadful subsequent record, and I marked down JOHN FERNELEY with this in mind. He did not win again in 2000, though he was second in the Royal Hunt Cup, a lot better than most Lincoln winners. 07 April 2000 AINTREE John Hughes Trophy 2m 6f handicap chase Going: good

In most years the pattern that 10/10 winners were rated within 10 pounds of Racing Post's top mark excludes about one-third of the runners, and there is not much form. This year, the restrictions were higher, and there was a form choice. 19/24 (79%) of the runners were excluded. Of the remaining 5 runners only the following had won a handicap:

D winners (2m 2f+)

IN THE BLOOD	12/99	Warwick 2m 3f	NWG
NORTHERN STARLIGHT	01 April	Ascot 2m 3^{1}/2f	
STORM DAMAGE	11/99	Chepstow 2m 3f	NW since
SUPREME CHARM	6 February	Leicester	poor jumper

In his previous race, NORTHERN STARLIGHT had been hard driven and in the end won gamely, RP commenting that he was an 'exceptionally tough' horse. National Hunt horses tend to be tougher than their Flat counterparts, and since he had not made any jumping mistakes, I thought that he could win again, which he did.

There were two FPFs. SUPREME CHARM was a poor jumper, as on his most recent victory he had made mistakes. At least he was a plausible favourite, having run well at the Cheltenham Festival, but why did punters make RISK OF THUNDER joint favourite? He had an excellent record over the specialist cross-country course at Punchestown, but nothing over steeplechase fences. I was rather puzzled at first, till by chance I looked at a part of the racing card which is irrelevant to my system. The owner's name was Sean Connery. 08 April 2000 AINTREE Cordon Bleu 2m handicap hurdle Going: good The statistical pattern tells you to look among the 5 y o and 6 y o runners carrying 10st 12lbs or less. Eliminating four on that basis, left four to consider, of which only two had any recent form in a handicap over the distance: D winners

DEE PEE TEE CEE 01 March Wetherby SHARPATEN 03 February Leopardstown DEE PEE TEE CEE had won at Wetherby, but 'hard pressed, driven out', so I thought that my rating of -10 suggested that this was a tougher race. SHARPATEN (trained by P Hughes), recommended by Craig Thake as the likely winner, was a complete enigma. He had won easily in his previous race, but had been raised 30 pounds by the handicapper. Sometimes you hear a trainer complain if one of his charges is raised by 10 pounds, but not P Hughes. I did not know what to make of this before the race, and was even more puzzled after SHARPATEN won quite easily at 16-1.

08 April 2000 AINTREE Red Rum handicap chase 2m
Going: good

In its own grisly way, this race did conform to a pattern. Despite the more than adequate prize money (£30,000) it attracted a small and feeble field (of seven runners), only one of which (SAMAKAAN) had any worthwhile form. I was not yet convinced that his trainer, Venetia Williams, could always be relied on in the big handicaps, so I decided to put SAMAKAAN on the 'monitor' list. SAMAKAAN was held by the winner, JUNGLI, who had won last time out, but in a 3 runner handicap at Newbury over 2m 1f which the Racing Post report had described as 'a fairly meaningless affair'.

08 April 2000 AINTREE Grand National 4m 4f chase
Going: good

This is a 'trappy' race, and if you must bet, look at the runners within the weight (10st 8lbs and below) and rating (142-155) trends, and apply a pin carefully! This was a slightly unusual year. Only 7 of the 40 runners were out of the handicap proper, whereas usually the proportion is much higher. 20 runners were eligible in terms of weight, and 10 in the ratings band.

The winner, PAPILLON, was in the weight group, at 10st 2lbs, but, rated 139, below the usual rating. He had not won a handicap chase before this race.

15 April 2000 AYR Scottish Grand National 4m 1f chase
Going: good

This was as difficult a race as ever, because of the distance. It was a poor quality field, because 13 of the 21 runners were out of the handicap.

If you had to make a selection in this trappy race, three horses seemed to be possibles. SCOTTON GREEN had won the Tote Northern National, Newcastle, over the same distance, but had reached his limit last time out in the Midlands Grand National. YOUNG KENNY won the same race in 1999, but prefers soft (today's going was good). PARIS PIKE had won over 3m 2f at Uttoxeter in good style, but this distance was 7f further than he had ever raced. There couldn't be a bet. PARIS PIKE won in good style at an unrealistically short price (5-2).

22, 24 April KEMPTON Easter meeting

The meeting continued on its downward path in 2000, with no big handicaps worthy of the name. The Rosebery Handicap over 10f, still a good middle-distance handicap in the mid 1990s, was quietly downgraded to a fairly average 8f handicap. None of the other handicaps was worth considering. The early part of the season, up to Royal Ascot, used to be quite full of valuable and well-contested handicaps at the metropolitan courses: the City and Sub-urban, Epsom; the Jubilee Cup, Kempton; the Whitsun Cup, Sandown; the London Gold Cup, Newbury. The Epsom races went a generation ago, but the others have tailed off very rapidly within the last five years. A sorry sight.

24 April FAIRYHOUSE Irish Grand National 3m 5f chase
Going: good to yielding

This is a trappy race, as the result confirmed. COMMANCHE COURT (7-11-4) had never won a chase, and his last win was in December 1998. There were two FPFs, ACKZO, put back from a 4m 2f win at Uttoxeter; and ED-MOND, who had not win since December 1999.

29 April SANDOWN Whitbread Cup 3m 5f chase
Going: good to soft

In chapter 4, I cautioned that this is a trappy race. As usual, the statistical trends (no 7 year old winners; weight below 10st 5lbs) allowed you to elim-inate 7 of the 20 runners, but this race has no form pattern, so it should al-ways be avoided.

There was a counter-trend FPF, BEAU, 'wrong' on two of the statistical trends, weight (10st 9lbs) and age (7). Furthermore, he was still a novice, and, had a dubious form record given his sketchy jumping last time out. Even the brilliant N A Twiston-Davies had placed him out of his depth here.

Or so I thought, when I watched the 'wrong' horse put up the right kind of performance. He made virtually all the running to win very impressively in-deed.

03 May ASCOT Victoria Cup 7f
Going: good to soft

Like most of the other metropolitan handicaps, this race is perhaps only in this book as a mark of courtesy to its distinguished past. It falls into the cat-egory of 'possible' winners, i.e. horse which ran well without winning, last time out. Although I think you should avoid betting on such horses, I always look to see if a leading stable has a runner of this kind. The only such train-er in today's race, I A Balding, entered EASTER OGIL, but he had not a glim-mer of worthwhile form.

The winner at 25-1, BOLD KING, had last won in August 1999, and had then been held off his present mark of 86. The result may have been a shock, but it was not a surprise. Nor was the poor performance of CARIBBEAN MONARCH, an FPF at 11-4. He had never won a handicap, but the magic name of Sir Michael Stoute on the racecard was enough to convince punters that he could. Although it was reported that he 'found disappointingly little' in this race, the punters were right in the longer term, as next time out he won the Royal Hunt Cup.

04 May PUNCHESTOWN Weatherbys Hurdle 2m

Going: good

Not a big handicap in terms of prize money, but the Punchestown Festival races are always big in terms of competition.

Just over half the 21 runners had not won a handicap, but enough of the remainder had form to guarantee a competitive race. At the distance there were four contenders:

C/D winnners

| DOUBLE ACCOUNT | 3/2000 | Punchestown 2m | h.o.t.m. |
| SHINY BAY 1 | 3 February | Punchestown 2m (held by KILLULT- |
| AGH STORM l.t.o.) |

D winners

| KILLULTAGH STORM | 25 April | Fairyhouse | |
| MAGUA | 12/99 | Leopardstown | NW since |

KILLULTAGH STORM had won a much more valuable race at Fairyhouse last time out. His trainer, W P Mullins, does well on his home turf and has a good record at Punchestown. No reflection on the odds compilers, but betting forecasts are not much of a guide to the market in Irish racing. MAGUA was 12-1 in the morning, and 4-1 favourite just before the off. Given that she had not won for 5 months, I thought that she could be identified as a clear false-priced favourite. KILLULTAGH STORM won well at a generous 7-1.

05 May NEWMARKET Rowley Mile H & K Commissions 7f handicap

Going: good

The 7f Newmarket races are the only type of big handicap where you can ignore the name of the trainer. A course and distance win is, of course, essential.

It was a straightforward race to analyse, as only RAYYAAN had winning form over the distance so early in the season. Most importantly, he was a course and distance winner, and, exceptionally, the name of the trainer is irrelevant. The favourite, STRAHAN, was one of my favourite types of FPF. Trained by John Gosden, he had won a 6f race earlier in the season, but last time out had just failed to catch RAYYAAN over the course and distance. Even the brilliant Gosden cannot buck this trend - a 'can reverse the form' is the best, i.e. most likely to lose, type of favourite.

In a very close run race RAYYAAN beat STRAHAN by a short head, winning at 11-2. STRAHAN continued to be a punters' favourite, and was an

FPF in 3 more races, the Wokingham (23 June), the Bunbury Cup (13 July), and a handicap at Goodwood (26 August).

10 May CHESTER Chester Cup 2m 2f 147y handicap
Going: good to firm

The 2000 renewal of this race fully confirmed my suggestion in chapter 3 that this is a very trappy handicap. The trends indicated the elimination of 1 runner in terms of rating (RAINBOW HIGH, on 113), and 5 in terms of age (including TOP CEES, who won this race in 1995 and 1997). None of the remaining 13 runners had won a race this season, so it was not much use to know that RAINBOW HIGH was a counter-trend FPF at 9-2. The winner, BANGALORE, had never won a handicap.

27 May 2000 THE CURRAGH CBA Handicap 10f
Going: yielding to soft

Not a great race in terms of prize money (£8280), but, like Newmarket, every race at The Curragh is a big handicap. Only course and distance winners have a chance here, leaving just three to consider: C/D winners

OSPREY RIDGE same race 1999 VISCARIA 01 May 2000

In handicap terms, OSPREY RIDGE (trained by Kevin Prendergast) was rated -2 and VISCARIA -8. OSPREY RIDGE had raced twice this season, winning over 9f at Navan, and then ran unplaced over too long a distance (12f) at Leopardstown. He was also suited by the yielding-soft going, whereas VISCARIA had only won on much softer going, and could be discounted.

Kevin Prendergast is a good trainer for this type of race, and was confident enough to tell his owner to book the victory celebrations in advance. He was quite right, and OSPREY RIDGE won at 7-2. VISCARIA was a perfectly reasonable favourite (at 5-2) but was always held by the winner.

OSPREY RIDGE won quite well, with ROYAL MIDYAN and VISCARIA filling the minor places: quite a testimony to the formful character of the Curragh.

20 June 2000 ROYAL ASCOT Duke of Edinburgh 12f handicap
Going: good to firm

This is one of my favourite races of the meeting, as it carries a double advantage. The trends are clear, making it possible to pick the winner; and a good winner from a top stable usually does well in his next handicap or two. So this is a race to weigh up carefully and to watch closely.

Five of the 20 runners had not won a handicap, and could be immediately eliminated; a further 5 had won over a longer distance, and could also be excluded. WESTENDER had won over 10f, but not this season, so he too could be left out. NATIONAL ANTHEM, trained by Sir Michael Stoute, had won a 10f race at Newmarket in May. My attention was caught by the SPOTLIGHT comment that '(the) trainer has won the last two runnings of this race with similar types', leading me to go back to check the record. In fact the comment was misleading, because Sir Michael Stoute's winners were not 'similar types'. In 1998 GREEK PALACE had not won this season; and in 1999 BLUEPRINT had won last time out over 12, not 10, furlongs. The four winners of the race in the 1990s with previous form had all won over 12 furlongs. On this basis, I decided that NATIONAL ANTHEM would be a 'counter-trend' FPF. There was also a slight concern about his mark. Now to look at the remaining 8, the qualifiers.

C/D winners

RADA'S DAUGHTER	7/99		NWTS

D winners

APRIL STOCK	29 May	Chepstow	outclassed here
CARLYS QUEST	19 May	Newbury	h.o.t.m.
GALLERY GOD	05 June	Thirsk	outclassed here
KATIYKHA	10/99	Newmarket	
RAIN IN SPAIN	7/99	Windsor	NWTS
WILLIE CONQUER	6/99	Brighton	NWTS
ZALAL	10/98	York	not won since 1998

I had a closer look at KATIYKHA. He had won his final race (12f Newmarket) of the 1999 season in good style and, this season, had won a Listed race at Gowran Park last time out. I am sure that Luca Cumani had KATIYKHA in mind for this race after his Newmarket win. Unfortunately, because of the trainer's dispute with the Aga Khan, KATIYHA was transferred to a very capable Irish trainer, John Oxx. However, as far as my records went, he was an unknown quantity in handicap racing over here, so I cautiously decided to put him on the 'monitor' list.

The magic of the knighted trainer's name bewitched the punters into making NATIONAL ANTHEM an absurdly short-priced favourite at 5-2. KATIYKHA's price of 10-1 was equally absurd, the only difference being that he won quite easily, with NATIONAL ANTHEM fourth.

21 June ROYAL ASCOT Ascot Stakes 2m 4f handicap
Going: good to firm

Ascot often seems to rely on cachet rather than cash to attract large fields. Today's race offered the lowest prize (£29,900) for a handicap at the meeting, less than half the prize for the Chester Cup.

No less than half the 24 runner field carried 9st 1lbs and above, with the top mark of 90 being awarded to BANGALORE. As the racing press euphemistically puts it, a field of 'largely moderate' animals. M C Pipe fielded 3 runners, one of which, HERO'S FATAL, caught the punter's fancy, perhaps because of his win at Deauville in 1998, to be a ludicrous 9-4 favourite. Subsequent events showed that this might have been Plan A, because he was unlucky in the Northumberland Plate and won the Cesarewitch convincingly. Today, he had to give way to BARBA PAPA, trained by the enigmatic A J Martin. In 1997, for Luca Cumani, he had won an apprentice maiden at Folkestone and 2 stakes races in Italy. In his most recent run, 2 months previously, he had won a non-handicap hurdle over 2m at Roscommon. Truly a 'dark' horse!

21 June ROYAL ASCOT Royal Hunt Cup 8f handicap
Going: good to firm

A race to avoid, as the usual form guidelines, particularly about distance, are of no help. This is such a difficult race that I would not even be confident about identifying a wrongly-priced favourite. In other races, this year's favourite, TILLERMAN, would have been an obvious FPF since he had not won this season. Nothing can be ruled out in the Hunt Cup, so that you couldn't say that TILLERMAN was without a chance. In the 1990s, this was a 'possible' race for a runner in the Victoria Cup (see 03 May). This year, CARIBBEAN MONARCH, had run disappointingly in that race, but succeeded here. He conformed to the usual 'pattern' of the race: he had not won this season, and had never won a handicap.

22 June ROYAL ASCOT King George V 12f 3 y o handicap
Going: good to firm

As I point out in chapter 3, the only form indicator to this race is to have won a handicap over this distance last time out. This year there were no qualifiers.

If you prefer to be more speculative, I have suggested that non-handicap winners from the best stables, which had won over 10f last time out, had a very good record. Just for the record, as I would not recommend this approach to finding winners, this year there were five possibles:

AIR DEFENCE	09 May	Chester	10.5f	B W Hills
BALDAQUIN	01 June	Goodwood	10f	Gosden
BUCKMINSTER	15 May	Redcar	10f	Gosden
COVER UP	10 April	Windsor	10f	Stoute
WATER JUMP	07 May	Salisbury	10f	Dunlop

Of these, AIR DEFENCE and WATER JUMP could be discounted, because they had to be hard ridden to win their maiden race, leaving them little in hand for their promotion to a major handicap. COVER UP's weight of 9st 1lbs and mark of 92 went against the trend of winning non-handicappers in this event. This left the two horses trained by Gosden. In the past decade his record was excellent, with three shrewd entries giving two winners and one placed horse. At this point, the difficulty of weighing up non-handicap form becomes apparent. How to decide between BALDAQUIN and BUCKMIN-STER? I suppose that BALDAQUIN would have to be the choice, since Goodwood form is usually a stone better than Redcar. However, to me this seems to me only a pound or two in advance of the selection-by-sticking-a-pin method. If you had to choose, and I would rather sit in a Labour Party focus group for a night and a day, then it would be BALDAQUIN.

The winner was GIVE THE SLIP, rated 95, had not won a handicap and carrying 9st 4lbs, trained by Mrs. A.J. Perrett, the daughter of former handicap maestro Guy Harwood. He had to be rousted out here, and so was not one for the notebook for Goodwood.

22 June 2000 ROYAL ASCOT Britannia Stakes 8f 3 y o handicap
Going: good to firm

The rule never to back non-handicap winners can be broken, but only as frequently as a politician keeps his promises! This is one of the exceptions, as the previous record of the race shows that it is best to back the trainer rather than form. For this race, look very carefully at runners from the leading stables which won last time out at the distance. Henry Cecil's entries are the most difficult to assess, for they really are 'dark horses', without any decipherable form. Fortunately he had given the race a miss, so I could concentrate on the only two qualifiers:

EL GRAN PAPA winner of an 8f maiden at Newbury, trained by J H M Gosden

SIGN OF HOPE winner of an 8f handicap at Pontefract trained by I A Balding.

I thought that as an entry for a major Royal Ascot handicap SIGN OF HOPE rather lived up to his optimistic name, and would be outclassed. Compared to the previous winners (NORTH SONG 1996; PLAN B 1998), which had reached this race by rather a devious route, EL GRAN PAPA seemed to be set on the fast track to victory. He had won comfortably over the distance last time out and was placed at exactly the right point in the handicap, on a mark of 85. In the 1990s, all the winners of this event which had not previously won a handicap were rated 84-94.

His chance was just as obvious to the betting public at large as it was to me, so there was never any sign of a false-priced favourite. EL GRAN PAPA was always a well-backed, but backable, favourite at 4-1. Although he won quite readily, winners of the Britannia usually aim to transfer to the supposedly more exalted sphere of Listed events. My expectation that I would not be able to back EL GRAN PAPA in another handicap was confirmed. SIGN OF HOPE ran well until beaten at the last gasp.

23 June 2000 ROYAL ASCOT Wokingham 6f handicap
Going: good to firm

The Wokingham makes the Royal Hunt Cup look like a model of predictability. It is the race to avoid par excellence. The winner, HARMONIC WAY, had not won this season, and seemed held off this mark, as last time out he was second off 101, one pound lower. He was a good, if academic, illustration of an important point about sprint handicaps. Some horses really do need an insane pace and a large field to show their best. In 1999 HARMONIC WAY had won the Stewards Cup under exactly those conditions, which he did not meet again until today's race.

The first five home were drawn 28, 17, 26, 29, 21, so I had a look at the odd man out, TUSSLE. Trained by M L W Bell, he had run well from a poor draw, but what this meant we shall never know, as his only other race in 2000 was over 7f.

Punters persisted, rather hopelessly in my view, with STRAHAN, making him an FPF, despite the fact that he was clearly held off his current mark.

ROYAL ASCOT meeting

It is a sign that 2000 was a slightly atypical year, that there were no winners or placed horses from leading stables which could be worth keeping in mind for the Goodwood July meeting.

01 July NEWCASTLE Northumberland Plate 2m handicap
Going: firm

After boosting the prize money for this race to £75000, only £3000 less than the Cesarewitch, it must have been rather disappointing for the Newcastle executive to see the rather ordinary field of handicappers which turned out for this event. Martin Pipe has a good record in this race, but on the form record you could not select his runner, HERO'S FATAL. He had not won a Flat handicap, and last time out had rather a hard race over 2m 4f at Royal Ascot. The winner, BAY OF ISLANDS, was an 8 year old rated 90 who had not won a race this season. He ran on well enough, but his connections were fortunate to pick up such a good prize.

08 July HAYDOCK Old Newton Cup 12f handicap
Going: good to firm

There was no qualifier from Royal Ascot this year, and it was rather a weak renewal. Although the prize money was about 5% more than the 12f handicaps at Royal Ascot, it was not apparently enough of a temptation for owners/trainers to venture north of Newmarket.

13 July NEWMARKET July Course Bunbury Cup 7f handicap
Going: good

This is a trappy race. The only worthwhile statistics (that 3 and 4 y os do well, and the race usually goes to an exposed handicapper carrying more than 8st 12lbs) did not really help. As usual, despite the fair prize of £26,000 at a very fashionable meeting, the race was ignored by most of the leading stables. There were no course and distance winners with recent form.

If only (the two most used words in horse racing) there had been a selection, because there were two obvious FPFs in the field. STRAHAN was held by RAYYAAN (see 05 May) off a mark of 91, and was now on 101; TILLERMAN had not won this season.

The winner, TAYSEER, confounded the statistical trends. As a 6 y o, he was outside the age group; and carried only 8st 9lbs. At least the race confirmed two negative form trends. TAYSEER had not won this season, and was put back in distance from 8f. He turned out to be one of those rare but irritating horses, rather like GRANGEVILLE, the 1999 winner, which could win good handicaps over both 6f and 7f. The only course-and-distance winner, SECOND WIND, failed to make an impression.

15 July YORK John Smith's Cup 10f 85 y handicap
Going: good

This was rather a poor quality field for such a lucrative prize. Sometimes there is a good handicapper in this race, and the absence of such a contender today was all the more galling, given that there was a classic FPF. MEDICEAN, trained by Sir Michael Stoute, had not won a handicap, but was beaten only a length by the high class Group horse, GIANT'S CAUSEWAY, last time out. He was also running from a very difficult draw (high). The comment ran along the lines 'close up third so will be so much higher in future handicaps'. MEDICEAN finished well-beaten, and the winner SOBRIETY had not won a handicap: pretty much what you would expect from such an uninspiring event.

02 August 2000 GALWAY Galway Plate 2m 6f handicap chase
Going: good to yielding

In about half the runnings of this race, there are horses with good form credentials. But not in 2000, as the only two horses with some claims could be discounted on other grounds:

MOSCOW EXPRESS	same race 1999	mistake l.t.o.
TREBLE BOB CD	winner 1998	NW since 9/1998

MOSCOW EXPRESS had always been prone to make small mistakes, but I thought that in a big race these would find him out. In the end it all turned out to be a farce, as the last two fences were omitted. In the circumstances, any runner could have won and DOVALI (at 20-1) did.

04 August GALWAY O'Malley Memorial 2m 1f handicap chase
Going: good

Not a very valuable prize (£10,700), but every race at the Galway Festival is the subject of fierce competition. There was no form in the Racing Post, so this is one of the occasions when the Irish racing website (www.irishfield.com) is absolutely invaluable.

There was only one runner with any recent form, FRANCIS BAY. He had won handicaps over today's distance at Ballinrobe (13 June) and Killarney (18 July), before being aimed too high for a 5 year old at the Galway Plate, where he finished seventh in rather messy race (see above, 02 August). He had won a 2m non-handicap hurdle at the Galway Festival in 1999, so he was well suited by the course. All this and Dermot Weld, the Galway maestro!

The Racing Post betting forecast of 7-4 seemed, if anything, rather generous. To my great surprise, RIVER CORA, who had not won a handicap, was made equal 3-1 favourite with FRANCIS BAY. Perhaps backers were influenced by the comment of the pre-race VERDICT column that after RIVER CORA won a conditions chase here '...it was interesting to learn afterwards that Willie Mullins is planning to run him in several big-value handicaps.'

Under a superlative ride by Paul Carberry, FRANCIS BAY won very easily. Readers should note Weld's comment that he thought he might make a Galway Plate winner in the future.

GOODWOOD JULY MEETING

A very disappointing meeting, as there were no selections in the big handicap races. In most years, there are one or two firm selections, although 1998 was also a blank year. I was not surprised, because the usual source of winners, Royal Ascot, had dried up in 2000. Nor were there any qualifiers from Newmarket or Sandown.

05 August GOODWOOD Stewards' Cup 6f handicap
Going: good

The Stewards Cup is a good example of a race which does follow a pattern (running well in the Wokingham at Royal Ascot, or high-class winning form), but is still difficult to solve. This year there were no horses with good form in the Wokingham at Royal Ascot. In fact, there were very few runners with recent form. Within the statistically significant ratings band of 91-103, the only qualifiers were: BLUE MOUNTAIN 2 July Goodwood

TAYSEER winner of the Bunbury Cup (see above, 13 July)

BLUE MOUNTAIN had won the Stewards Cup Trial, but I thought that he would be outclassed here. TAYSEER had been beaten over 7f last time out, off the same mark (93), and his form record over 6f was discouraging enough: 3145050. If you are a fan of D Nicholls as a trainer, (undoubtedly he is very good with sprint handicappers), then you might have selected TAYSEER, but I could not see him winning. Win he did, at 6-1, with BLUE MOUNTAIN a well beaten 5-1 favourite.

23 August 2000 YORK Ebor 14f handicap
Going: good

This year, the Ebor was the richest prize (£113,750) for Flat stayers in Europe, non-handicaps included. Looking at the two key pointers, the draw and the entries of the leading trainers, the short list was as follows:

ALVA GLEN (Stoute)	3-8-10	**rated 103**
BIENNALE (Stoute)	**not won a race this season**	
BOREAS (Cumani)	5-9-0	**rated 95**

In my book, ALVA GLEN and BOREAS were both rated -5, i.e. on level terms. ALVA GLEN, drawn 11, was just outside the favoured low draw of 1-10, while BOREAS was well drawn at 7. On one of the key statistical trends, BOREAS had the edge, and as the Ebor often falls to a 'dark' horse, I wondered if he fitted into that category. Thanks to the Racing Post website, I soon found out that he certainly was. He did not run as a 2 year old, had a serious leg injury in the following season, and this was only his seventh race.

Luca Cumani had been pretty open about his chances, and so in the biggest handicap of the season, with 22 runners, he started at 11-4f, a totally daft price.

The race confounded one of the main trends. The winner, GIVE THE SLIP (trained by Mrs. A J Perrett), was unfavourably drawn (16), but Eddery rode a brilliant race by bringing GIVE THE SLIP right over to a pole position, to beat BOREAS by three-quarters of a length. After winning the King George V (see above, 22 June), GIVE THE SLIP had run reasonably well in a 12f Listed race at Goodwood. Although the programme mapped out for GIVE THE SLIP was not an obvious one, this was a fine piece of training by Mrs. Perrett, so I made a note to check her record at the end of the season. In the three seasons to 2000, she had trained 7, 18 and 25 winners respectively, which suggested that she would be a force in the future in big handicaps.

Looking back through my records for the season, I noted that she had also won the Chester Cup, with BANGALORE. The horse had been bought out of B W Hills stable at the end of 1999, won 2 small hurdle races, and then ran a close-up third in one of the handicaps which sometimes has a bearing on the Chester race. An astute training performance, firstly to make something out of a horse bought from one of the shrewdest trainers in business, and then to win a big prize in a race usually ignored by the leading trainers.

26 August 2000 NEWMARKET July Course Chris Blackwell Memorial 7f handicap
Going: good to firm

As a reminder: the 7f Newmarket races are the only type of big handicap where you can ignore the name of the trainer. A course and distance win is, of course, essential.

Although half of the 16 runners had either not won a handicap or a race, it was still competitive enough.

C/D winners

CELEBRATION TOWN	05 July		

D winners

ATAVUS	5/00	Newmarket	NW since May
COWBOYS AND ANGELS	17 July	Ayr	held off 74 l.t.o., now 76
SUMTHINELSE	28 June	Chester	held by CELEBRATION TOWN
TRIBAL PRINCE	18 August	Folkestone	outclassed here
WILLOUGHBYS BOY	19 July	Yarmouth	h.o.t.m.

CELEBRATION TOWN was the clear selection on form. He seemed to go well (3 wins out of 5) for his new stable, D Morris, and for his jockey, Ray Cochrane. However, against the general weather pattern this Flat season, the going turned good to firm, causing his trainer to withdraw CELEBRATION TOWN, so there was no selection.

03 September 2000 THE CURRAGH Cambridgeshire 8f handicap
Going: good to firm

The only course and distance winner was SILVERWARE, but he had no chance on form, since his last win was in June 1999. Trained to perfection, he won in good style.

06 September 2000 DONCASTER Portland 5f 140y handicap
Going: good to firm

This is a race with fairly clear trends: horses rated 84+. However, in 2000 this trend only ruled out 3 of 22 runners. The record shows that 6f winners are favoured, so I confined my analysis to winners over that distance or CD winners.

C/D winners

CADEAUX CHER	same race 1998	h.o.t.m.

D (6f) winners

BOLD EFFORT	6/00	Salisbury	
BRECONGILL LAD	9/99	Goodwood	h.o.t.m.
CRY HAVOC	7/00	Epsom	h.o.t.m.
FURTHER OUTLOOK	6/99	psom	NWTS
HO LENG	9/99	York	NWTS
LAGO DI VERANO	7 August	Ripon	h.o.t.m.
MAGIC RAINBOW	5/99	Kempton	(winning since over 5f)
DEPERDINE	6/99	York	NWTS

Elimination left only BOLD EFFORT, who won last time out at Bath over 5.5f. Not exactly top-class form, and I did not consider his trainer to be in the big league, so I could not see a selection in this race. The winner, COMPTON BANKER, conformed to the weight, age and rating trend (3-8-8, rated 89), and negatively confirmed the distance trend, that a 5f horse can win this race when unopposed by a good class 6f winner.

16 September 2000 AYR Gold Cup 6f handicap
Going: soft, heavy patches

The going was soft, with heavy patches, so it was blindfold time. But just for practice, I decided to look through the 29 runner field. TAYSEER had won the Stewards Cup very well, and, as winners of this race come from anywhere in the ratings, it did not matter that he was quite highly rated, at 102. But as a 6 y o, he was in the wrong age group for this race, so I immediately discounted his chance. Looking through the favoured age group of three and four year olds, the only runner which seemed worth a second glance was LORD PACAL, trained by Neville Callaghan. He was a winner last time out at Newmarket, but over 7f, so I ruled him out.

The winner, BAHAMIAN PIRATE, was a 33-1 shock. It is true that he had won a 6f handicap at Newmarket (11 August), but he was then well held in the Great St. Wilfrid off 84, for which he had been raised 2 pounds. I was disappointed that there could be no selection, as there was a ludicrously false-priced favourite. GAELIC STORM's only win this season was in a 3 runner non-handicap at Klampenborg. At the time, I asked myself, where? By chance, I visited it a month later. It is a beautiful seaside resort just outside Copenhagen; but not such an attractive guide to the most valuable sprint handicap of the season.

20 September 2000 LISTOWEL Kerry National 3m handicap chase
Going: soft to heavy

The greatly increased prize money attracted several horses with recent form.

2m 4f - 3m winners

DUINN	6/2000	Cork 3m	h.o.t.m.
INS CARA	12/99	Leopardstown 3m	NW since 12/99
LAAZIM AFOOZ	12 August	Stratford 3m	outclassed here
MAC'S SUPREME	25 June	Perth 3m	outclassed here
SCALLYBUCK 21	July	Kilbeggan	h.o.t.m.
THE DELL	06 September	Galway	2m 6f

Elimination left only THE DELL. The big question was the going, as the softest going over which THE DELL had won was yielding-soft. The going was soft to heavy, and, in the west of Ireland, that is just what it means, i.e. much more testing than THE DELL had ever previously faced. His trainer, Miss F M Crowley, is very competent, but I have found that only the most outstanding trainers can judge whether or not a horse can handle different types of going. To win a big prize with MAC'S SUPREME after a rather lucky victory at a minor Scottish course, his trainer, Ferdy Murphy, is proving to be shrewdness personified. THE DELL was a well-beaten fourth.

23 September 2000 ASCOT Tote 7f handicap
Going: good to soft

This is a race for 'possible' horses, i.e. those which have shown promising form, either by winning or staying on well at a different distance or type of course. Not the category of horse in which I am interested, but if you are, it could be stretched to include the winner, DUKE OF MODENA. His trainer, G B Balding, rarely gets the right kind of ammunition, and, if my memory serves me right, his last really top class handicapper was GREEN RUBY, winner in 1986 of the Stewards Cup, a York August handicap, and the Ayr Gold Cup.

The race did illustrate a point about the season falling into 'time zones'. RAYYAAN had won two 7f handicaps at Newmarket (see 05 May, above), but returning for an autumn campaign, found that he was now outgunned, even though the handicapper had relaxed his grip slightly.

24 September ASCOT Showcase (Ritz) 12f handicap
Going: soft

An early sign of the wettest autumn for 250 years, as the rains came down with the autumn equinox. The going changed quickly from good to soft, scuppering the chances of most of the runners with reasonable form.

C/D winners

RAISE A PRINCE	9/98	NW since;	PBD.
WAIT FOR THE WILL	July 2000	NWG	

D winners

FLOSSY	11/99	Doncaster	NWTS
LIGNE GAGNANTE	6/99	Goodwood	PBD
LIVIUS	27 August	Goodwood	NWG
MOWELGA	4/2000	Newmarket	held by TAKWIN
ROMANTIC AFFAIR	07 July	Salisbury;	PBD
SEEK	22 August	York	
SUMMER SONG	02 September	Thirsk	NWG
TAKWIN	09 September	Doncaster	NWG
ULUNDI	03 September	Kempton	NWG

As shown in the table above, all the 11 distance winners bar SEEK could be discounted, on various grounds. SEEK caught my attention since he was trained by Luca Cumani, and was in line with the trends for this race (his rating was 92, compared to the 10 year average of 91).

Not worth backing as 11-4 favourite, SEEK ran really badly to finish well down the field. The winner, KIND REGARDS, at least confirmed one of the trends, being rated 92, but had no reasonable form.

24 September 2000 ASCOT Mile Final handicap
Going: soft

TORNADO PRINCE's win in 2000 just about sums up the form worthiness of this race. His five career wins had all been on fast going (the going here was soft); he was rated 10 pounds higher than he had ever won a handicap; and his only win this season was in a 7f handicap at Thirsk. The result? he stormed home by 9 lengths. Definitely a race to avoid.

30 September 2000 NEWMARKET Rowley Mile Links 7f handicap
Going: good

Apart from the Bunbury Cup, the 7f handicaps at Newmarket are not big handicaps in terms of prize money, but are usually very competitive, with the leading trainers quite well represented. In this race, I looked for confirmation of a strong trend for winners of the 7f handicap at the Doncaster St. Leger meeting to win at Newmarket. This year NORFOLK REED, trained by R Hannon, had won there after a series of ordinary performances. Raised only 3 pounds for that win, in my book he was on level terms with the handicapper, so it was time to look at the opposition:

D winners

APLOY	7/00	Salisbury	h.o.t.m.
BOLDLY GOES	8/00	Newcastle	held by NORFOLK REED
DONNA'S DOUBLE	7/00	York	h.o.t.m.

REDSWAN	9/99	Doncaster	NWH this season SUPREME
SALUTATION	7/99	Catterick	held by NORFOLK REED
TOPTON	7/00	Yarmouth	held by NORFOLK REED
URSA MAJOR	9/99	York	NWTS

REDSWAN had won the 7f Doncaster St Leger meeting handicap in 1999, and then not run again until this season. Last time out, he had won a claiming race over the course and distance, and had been raised 7 pounds as a result. I ruled him out because he had not won a handicap this season.

NORFOLK REED seemed a straightforward selection, and a good bet with SUPREME SALUTATION being made favourite in the hope that he could reverse the form. However the SPOTLIGHT notes in the Racing Post commented that NORFOK REED '...may not be straightforward...claims if in the same mood.' There was something unconvincing about his form before the Doncaster meeting, but I decided that the trend should overcome my reservations.

My reservations proved justified, and NORFOLK REED ran an undistinguished race somewhere in the middle of the field. The winner was SEA MARK, a completely unpredictable 'dark horse', trained by B W Hills. He had won only one race, a 7f Leicester apprentice maiden, as a 3 y o in 1999; and had made no impression on his only run, in March.

30 September 2000 NEMARKET Rowley Mile Cambridgeshire 9f handicap

Going: good

As shown in chapter 2, this is a good race for trend-followers. As in every year, there was a large field and the task of making a shortlist was time consuming. Of the 35 runners, 8 could be immediately eliminated because they had not won a handicap. Then the list of winners over 7f (Doncaster), 8f and 10f is drawn up, as follows.

ATAVUS	5/00	Newmarket	NW since May
ATLANTIC RHAPSODY	5/00	Haydock	NW since May
BOMB ALASKA	5/99	Goodwood	NWTS
BOUND FOR PLEASURE	09 September	Doncaster	10.5f
BRILLIANT RED	7/99	Sandown	NWTS
CHAPEL ROYALE	7/00	Newmarket	h.o.t.m.
DANCING KRIS	8/99	Deauville	NWTS
FANTAZIA	8/99	Newmarket	10fNWTS
FIRST FANTASY	10/99	Yarmouth 10f	outclassed
JATHAABEH	22 July	Newmarket 8f	
KATY NOWAITEE	04/00	Doncaster	NW since March
LADY ANGHARAD	07 July	Sandown	10f h.o.t.m.
MILLIGAN	04/00	Newmarket	10f h.o.t.m.
NOOSHMAN	7/00	Goodwood	10f h.o.t.m.

PYTHIOS	6/99	Ascot	NWTS
VINTAGE PREMIUM	4/00	Newbury	NW since April
WEET-A-MINUTE	10/95	York 85	NW since 1995

Of the 17 runners over the right distances, just two are not eliminated: -3 JATHAABEH
+8 BOUND FOR PLEASURE

The best-in horse, BOUND FOR PLEASURE, had won at the Doncaster St Leger meeting, as had 5 of the last 10 winners of this race. He was trained by John Gosden, whose horses were currently in great form. Everything seemed to fall in place: a horse with good recent form, in line with the trends, and trained by the best man for this kind of handicap. Even better, there was a false priced favourite, NOOSHMAN, trained by Sir Michael Stoute, which had lost his last three races and was firmly held off this mark.

In the race, BOUND FOR PLEASURE, the 11-2 joint favourite, could not make his mark and was never better than mid-division. The winner, KATY NOWAITEE had won at Doncaster, but at the first meeting of the season! This was a very good piece of training by P W Harris, as she had not raced since. Here she won in tremendous style, and proved herself in Listed company at the next Newmarket meeting.

30 September 2000 THE CURRAGH Cesarewitch 2m handicap
Going: soft

There were no course-and-distance winners with good recent form, so there was no selection. The win by TRAGIC LOVER represented an excellent feat of training by permit-holder, Donal Kinsella, in only his third race since joining the stable. His previous win was over 12f at The Curragh, but he had not won over the distance.

14 October 2000 NEWMARKET Rowley Mile Cesarewitch 2m 2f handicap
Going: soft

The race had a strange configuration for a Flat handicap, since 14 of the 33 runners were not in the handicap proper, signalling rather a poor quality field. There was a clear false-priced favourite, BARBA PAPA, trained by A J Martin, with rather an unusual reason for one of the longest handicaps in the programme: put back in distance, after winning the 2m 4f Ascot stakes. A J Martin had won the Cambridgeshire in 1999 with SHE'S OUR MARE, and racegoers were obviously expecting another shrewd thrust at winning a big handicap. TURNPOLE, trained by Mrs. Reveley, who had won this race in 1997 and, now an 8 y o, seemed to have lost his form recently and could not be fancied.

The race was a complete surprise to all bar, presumably, Martin Pipe and connections. The winner, HEROS FATAL, had not won since Deauville, August 1998, although he may have been unlucky in the Northumberland Plate when his saddle slipped. The result confirms the trend of the last decade for the race to be won by handicappers aged 5 y o and over. I looked carefully through the field to see if there were any horses of the type which used to do so well in this race up to the end of the 1980s - lightly raced three- or four-year olds in good stables which had won distance handicaps close to the date of the race - and there were none. The last horse of this kind was ORCHESTRA STALL, a 3 y o beaten for stamina in 1995. This change in the winning pattern must remain one of racing's mysteries, as £78,000 is always worth winning. The result dispelled any lingering inclinations to spend time unravelling the Cesarewitch in the future.

04 November 2000 DONCASTER November 12f handicap
Going: heavy

This is a key race for trend followers, so I hoped to end the Flat season with a good win. Unfortunately, in 2000 the rains poured down relentlessly, and the going on the Town Moor was bottomless. Just the recipe for a form upset, and so it turned out.

Only two runners had either won over course and distance, or at one of the courses (Haydock, Newmarket) which give a pointer to this race: FLOSSY won the same race in 1999; held by SEREN HILL l.t.o.

SEREN HILL 12 October Newmarket

SEREN HILL had just beaten FLOSSY at Newmarket in their previous race, and had not been too harshly re-rated by the handicapper. However he was at the end of his tether to win, and I could not see him winning again. FLOSSY was made a very short 5-2 favourite, on the 'can reverse the form' basis. Although she was a clear false-priced favourite, unfortunately I could not see any other horse with form credentials.

The winner, BATSWING, had won a 10.5 f handicap at Chepstow in June, off a mark 14 pounds lower. This was a form upset, as the big races in October and November usually go to a horse with good recent form. SEREN HILL was fourth, a good distance in front of FLOSSY, so at least that was a confirmation of my views on the plausibility of 'can reverse the form' favourites.

11 November CHELTENHAM Old Course Thomas Pink 2m 4 Ωf handicap chase
Going: good to soft

This is a trappy race, because it is too early in the season to weigh up the form and the distance preferences of most of the field. The only possible key is recent Cheltenham form or a good showing at the Festival meeting, and none of today's runners fell into that category.

Although she was trained by M C Pipe, I still thought that LADY CRICKET was an FPF, since she had not won a handicap. Fortunately there was nothing to back in opposition, as she won quite well.

25 November NEWBURY Hennessy Gold Cup 3m 2$\frac{1}{2}$f handicap chase
Going: good to soft
The 2000 running of the race highlights the conflict between trend and trainers. The trend ran strongly in favour of KINGSMARK: an improving 7 year old who had won the Edward Hanmer (Haydock 3m chase) in good style, for which he was lightly burdened by a 4 pounds penalty (+1 in my handicap). He also had a good form chance, as only STRONG TEL had won over anything near the distance, and half the field could be immediately discounted for various reasons. KINGSMARK seemed to have an outstanding chance, but in my view his trainer, Martin Todhunter, was so far unproven at this level. Given that the record showed that 8/10 winners were from leading stables, it was better to treat this as more of a race for assessing the trainer than for backing the horse.

As the race turned out, that was the crucial trend, since the winning trainer was N Twiston-Davies with KING'S ROAD. He was within the age and ratings bands, but had not previously won a handicap chase. Perhaps this was an unusual result, since all 10 previous winners had won handicaps before this race. The fact that the top weight was rated at 154 indicated that this was a weaker race than usual, as in most years the top mark is well into the 160s.

There was an interesting post-mortem of the race by Topspeed (James Willoughby) in the Racing Post (29 November 2000). His figures showed that the Hennessy was run at a slow early pace, developing in the later stages to the nearest that a distance staying chase comes to being a sprint. This seems plausible, but I was not convinced by his argument that KINGSMARK had not had time to recover from his race in the Edward Hanmer. Previous winners of the Hennessy had run in that race at a closer interval, and it had not seemed to matter. The key factor, as Willoughby also pointed out, is the going: if the going is at least good/soft, then it does take a staying chaser more than two weeks to recover.

02 December SANDOWN William Hill 2m 110y handicap hurdle abandoned

The wettest autumn for centuries continued, and the two day programme at Sandown was abandoned. I did not consider this a great loss, since the National Hunt season is still spluttering into life, and the outlines of form are only beginning to take shape.

09 December CHELTENHAM New Course Tripleprint Gold Cup 2m 5f handicap chase
Going: soft

The statistical trends on age and handicap mark ruled out 5 of the 12 runners, without giving any further clues. In terms of form, half the field had not won a handicap chase, and 2 runners were put back in distance. This is a trappy race, because it is too early in the season for solidly established form to be available.

The result was a 'surprise'. GO ROGER GO confounded the statistical trends by being just below the ratings band of 134+, but negatively confirmed the form trends, since he had not won a handicap chase and had lost all his four completed runs at 2m 4f. At least the performance of the FPF, the unreliable jumper, EXIT SWINGER, was more predictable, as he finished down the field.

27 December 2000 CHEPSTOW Welsh National 3m 6f handicap chase
Going: soft

One of the outstanding form races, in which previous Chepstow form, particularly from the 3m Rehearsal Chase run at the beginning of December, works out splendidly.

The obvious candidate was MORAL SUPPORT, winner of that race, and trained by C J Mann. However, looking in detail at the race report, I noticed that he had hit the 14th fence. In a competitive race, such a blunder meant that he had to be ruled out. Certainly he was not a 5-2 favourite.

In a thrilling finish, he was outrun in the closing stages by JOCKS CROSS, whom he had beaten in the earlier race.

22 January 2001 HAYDOCK Peter Marsh 3m handicap chase
Abandoned

The second big handicap casualty of a harsh winter, regrettable because there is a reliable form/statistics pattern for this race.

27 January 2001 DONCASTER Great Yorkshire Chase 3m handicap chase
Going: good to soft

This was a race in which the statistics trend helped me to avoid picking a loser, although as it turned out the result contradicted the trend.

The statistics showed that all 8 out of the last 8 races (2 abandoned in the

1990s) were won by horses in the 127-142 band. They countered the form trend, that the race usually goes to a progressive type of horse which had won one of its previous 2 starts. There was such a horse in this race, KING ON THE RUN, trained by Venetia Williams. Last time out, he had won quite well over 2m 4f at Newbury, 2m 4Ωf at Kempton, after being bought out of another yard. He had shown good form on today's going the softish side of good.

However, rated 125, he fell 2 pounds outside the ratings band, and so was not a selection. The field seemed rather weak for a good prize (£31,850) and none of the others had any good recent form. Still, statistical trends are my rules, and KING ON THE RUN had to be passed over.

He ran quite a good race, being genuinely unlucky to be hampered twice, and, although he persisted on the run-in, he could not quite make up lost ground. The winner, HEIDI III, was a complete 20-1 shock, as he had not won a handicap chase, his best effort being second...in a three-runner field.

There was a baffling 100-30 FPF. AD HOC had fallen in his last two runs, and was put back in distance. The press comment sounded a proper note of caution: '...clearly needs to brush up his jumping having fallen on both starts since ((April))...has to be feared if putting in a clear round.' Never in contention, after this race his form figures read a discouraging FFP.

03 February 2001 SANDOWN Tote 2m 6f handicap hurdle
Going: heavy

Of the 21 runners, the weight and rating trends pointed to the elimination of 5. Only one horse fitted in with the form pattern for this race, of a win this season over 2m 4f+ at a good class course: THE EXTRA MAN. The only horse in the care of a leading trainer (N Henderson) with anything of a chance, was IRIS ROYAL, but scraping home at Fontwell was not much of an encouragement. Trained by M J Ryan, THE EXTRA MAN held on 'gamely, all out' to win at Cheltenham over 2m 5f on 12 November, before being beaten last time over an unsuitable 3m at Kempton. M J Ryan is a good Flat trainer, but rarely has enough high class N.H. horses to make a judgement about his ability, and I thought that THE EXTRA MAN had reached his limit at Cheltenham. Always be prepared for a surprising FPF. PATRAS was one of the four 7-1 favourites in the Racing Post, but on the course was a clear 13-2 favourite. His last win was on 19 February 2000, he had been beaten twice, and this was his first run this season. The Racing Post comments, '...off ten months but goes well fresh, promises to stay, good claiming amateur booked and still fairly treated...', added up to a series of plausible half-reasons, but in my view they made a solid case against PATRAS.

In a slugging finish in heavy going, THE EXTRA MAN just held off BAL-

LET K. His win was a textbook demonstration that superior jumping is just as important in hurdles as it is in steeplechases, as he was matched for sheer guts by the runner-up, but outpaced him over the hurdles.

Incidentally, Craig Thake ('Ten Year Trends', Racing Post) picked the winner, as he does many winners of big handicaps. I do feel that he gets far less credit for his thoughtful analysis of such races than he deserves. For instance, there was no mention of the fact in the next issue of Racing Post that he had just picked a 16-1 winner. When other tipsters do so, they rightly get a headline mention. In fact, if you haven't the time to analyse the big handicaps in depth, just read his column carefully, and see whether his selection meets the form/statistics pattern.

10 February 2001 NEWBURY Tote Gold Trophy 2m^{1}/2f handicap hurdle

Going: heavy

With the going just this side of waterlogged, ability to act on very heavy going was crucial. 21 runners turned out, but 9 could be immediately eliminated because they had not won a handicap hurdle. Of the remainder, the following 9 had won over the distance or over 2m 1f, and fell within the age (7 years old and younger) and rating (132-147) pattern. It is also interesting to note that M C Pipe, who had 6 runners in today's race, has had only one winner from 17 contestants.

COPELAND	12/99 Sandown	NW since
GRINKOV	14 January Leopardstown	NW heavy
HIT AND RUN	4/99 Warwick	NW since
HULYSSE ROYAL	12 November Cheltenham	
LANDING LIGHT	27 January Cheltenham	
MILLIGAN	10/00 Wetherby	NW since
RAINBOW FRONTIER	1/00 Ascot	NW since
THE FRENCH FURZE	1/00 Cheltenham	NW since

I thought that LANDING LIGHT (+1) had the edge over HULYSSE ROYAL (-4). In addition, the latter had been beaten by MR COOL (also in this race, but outside the rating band) last time out in a non-handicap. His trainer, O Sherwood, had not had a winner for over 6 weeks. By contrast, the ever-informative N Henderson had been irrepressibly bullish about LANDING LIGHT, almost a recommendation in its own right. I checked back his record on this bottomless going, and he had won once in these conditions.

I had hoped that the betting market might throw up an FPF, as some usually shrewd critics went for HULYSSE ROYAL (can reverse the form) and ROOSTER BOOSTER (not won a handicap hurdle). LANDING LIGHT was never better than 4-1 favourite, and won in the comfortable style predicted by his trainer.

17 February 2001 NEWCASTLE Tote Northern National 4m 1f handicap chase

Going: soft to heavy

The race has been dominated by lightweights, a trend which I expected to continue as the going turned heavy. It was an intriguing contest, as 4 of the 12 runner field had a chance of sorts.

MURT'S MAN, trained by P F Nicholls, could be anything. Although he had won at 3m 1^{1}/2f at Wincanton in impressive style, he was carrying 11-5 over a mile further, two major negatives against his chance this time. Mrs. Reveley's SEVEN TOWERS had won this race off a 6 pounds higher mark (122) in 1997, and carried a light weight, 11-1. However, he was now 12 years old, and had never shown his best form on this going. You can never overlook Twiston-Davies' runners, but LADY OF GURTMERRON carrying 10-10, was not a reliable jumper. If you look for 'possible' types, then SCOTTON GREEN would be your selection. The winner of this race off the same mark (110) last year, he was ideally suited by heavy going. Trained by T D Easterby, whose horses were in good form, he had not won this season but ran on well last time out. However, in my view, all four had varying sizes of question mark against their name, and there was no selection.

Surprisingly, given the Racing Post SP forecast of 5-1, SCOTTON GREEN was 5-2f, in my view a false price since he had not won this season. The race confirmed some of my analysis.

LADY OF GURTMERRON jumped badly from the beginning and soon lost her chance; and MURT'S MAN was nowhere to be seen. The battle for the minor placings was fought out between SCOTTON GREEN and SEVEN TOWERS. Both were well held by the novice, NARROW WATER, whose previous win was in a 3m 2f novice chase at Carlisle, where he had blundered badly at one fence. The winner was trained by Ferdy Murphy, who has quickly established a reputation with 'dark' horses in staying chases (see above, e.g. ACKZO, 18 March 2000; MAC'S SUPREME, 20 September 2000). This was certainly quite a performance, carrying 11st 5lbs on such heavy going.

24 February 2001 HAYDOCK De Vere Gold Cup 3m 4f handicap chase

Going: soft

Such are the vagaries of racing that, for exactly the same prize money (£58,000) as in the previous year, there was a much larger (18 runners compared to 7) and more competitive field.

I consider this to be rather a trappy race, as the winners come from a great range of distances. Haydock is a very testing course, both because of its up-hill finish and its tough fences, so it is difficult to find suitable preparatory races.

Only YOUNG KENNY had solid recent form. The winner of this race in 1999, he won at Aintree over 3m 3f in November 2000, but then was well held by STREAMSTOWN over 3m 1f at Wetherby on 11 January 2001. The latter was a 'dark' horse if ever I saw one. Although he had not jumped well when winning his second handicap, over 3m at Haydock on 25 November 2001, his Wetherby win was pretty fluent. What made him so intriguing was that he was trained by Ferdy Murphy, who over less than a year had shown himself very clever at winning long distance chases.

As I only bet on solid form, I decided that there was no selection. However, I thought I could see a clear FPF. Even N A Twiston-Davies could not win such a competitive race with a horse (FRANTIC TAN) which, in its last outing had jumped badly to win a 4 runner 3m novice chase at Newbury. The last time a novice had won this race was 1983. I thought wrong!. FRANTIC TAN ran off with this race, with STREAMSTOWN over 30 lengths away in 5th. For the second time in this year at the races (the first was BEAU, 29 April SANDOWN Whitbread Cup), see above, Twiston-Davies had trained a novice with chancy jumping to run away with a big handicap. Perhaps it is also worth noting that the only two winning FPFs this season turned up in 'trappy' races, which is usually the case.

24 February 2001 KEMPTON Racing Post Chase 3m handicap chase
Going: good to soft

Although course-and-distance winners have a good record in this race, I consider it a 'neutral' race, since runners with good recent form are the exception rather than the rule.

In today's race, there were two course and distance winners,:

EAU DE COLOGNE 27 December 2000

STRUGGLES GLORY 29 January 2001

The only other horse with good recent form was:

YOUNG SPARTACUS Cheltenham 2m 5f 27 February 2001

I could not rule out STRUGGLES GLORY on the grounds that he was a 10 year old, as runners from that age group have a respectable record. Cheltenham form is top-rate, and can be taken at any other course, so YOUNG SPARTACUS had to come into the picture. Here are my handicap marks:

-2 EAU DE COLOGNE

-3 YOUNG SPARTACUS

-9 STRUGGLES GLORY

They suggested that the race was between EAU DE COLOGNE and YOUNG SPARTACUS, who both had the edge on STRUGGLES GLORY. I was sorry to note that the trainers of both EAU DE COLOGNE and STRUGGLES GLORY were the subject of stories in the Racing Post of the 'small trainer can beat the big battalions' type, as this is usually the kiss of death to a horse's chances. However, I decided to put the trainer of EAU DE COLOGNE (Mrs L Richards) on the 'monitor' list.

EAU DE COLOGNE was withdrawn just before the race, leaving YOUNG SPARTACUS with a clear chance on form. He was trained by H D Daly, formerly an assistant to the much-missed Captain T A Forster. Daly had only been training since 1998, and since then he had shown with EDMOND that he could train the winner of a big handicap (the Welsh Grand National, 1999), so it would be interesting to see what he could do here.

YOUNG SPARTACUS fought out a tremendous finish to beat COMMANCHE COURT (most recent handicap win, the 3m 5f Irish Grand National in 2000). STRUGGLES GLORY, a reasonably-priced favourite at 11-4, ran on gamely into third place. A good training performance by H D Daly, enough to show that in the future he can be relied on to win big handicaps.

SELECTIONS / RACES MONITORED 2000

FPF = false-priced favourite

BEAU	**L 5-1 FPF**
RUBHAHUNISH	**W 8-1 FPF**
NORTHERN STARLIGHT	**W 7-1 FPF**
KILLULTAGH STORM	**W 7-1 FPF**
RAYYAAN	**W 11-2 FPF**
OSPREY RIDGE	**W 7-2f**
EL GRAN PAPA	**W 4-1f**
FRANCIS BAY	**W 3-1f**
CELEBRATION TOWN	withdrawn
SEEK	L 11-4f
NORFOLK REED	L 20-1
BOUND FOR PLEASURE	L 11-2f
LANDING LIGHT	**W 4-1f**

Races monitored

KINGSMARK	L 10-3f
MASTER TERN	W 9-2f
SAMAKAAN	L 10-11f
YOUNG SPARTACUS	W 9-1

As a quick reference to aid the reader, I have given a brief characterisation of every race, to identify those races which: regularly follow a strong form pattern (marked 'form') regularly follow a statistical trend ('statistics') follow form/statistics trends in 4/10 races ('neutral') should definitely be avoided ('trappy') regularly fall to 'dark' or 'possible' horses.

QUICK REFERENCE:
DATE ORDER
(sample dates, taken from Chapter 6 'season', 2000-2001)

2000
MARCH

14 Cheltenham: William Hill	neutral
14 Cheltenham: Ladbroke	statistics
15 Cheltenham: Coral trappy	
15 Cheltenham: Mildmay of Flete	statistics
16 Cheltenham: County	neutral
16 Cheltenham: Grand Annual	trappy
18 Uttoxeter: Midlands Grand National	neutral
25 Doncaster: Lincoln	trappy

APRIL

07 Aintree: John Hughes Memorial	statistics
08 Aintree: Cordon Bleu	statistics
08 Aintree: Red Rum	trappy
08 Aintree: Grand National	possible
15 Ayr : Scottish Grand National	trappy
24 Fairyhouse: Irish Grand National	trappy
29 Sandown: Whitbread Gold Cup	trappy

MAY

02-05 Punchestown Festival	meeting
03 Ascot: Victoria Cup	possible
10 Chester: Chester Cup t	rappy

JUNE

20 Royal Ascot: Duke of Edinburgh	form / statistics
21 Royal Ascot: Ascot stakes	trappy
21 Royal Ascot: Royal Hunt Cup	trappy
22 Royal Ascot: Britannia	dark
22 Royal Ascot: King George V	possible
23 Royal Ascot: Wokingham	trappy

JULY

01 Newcastle: Northumberland Plate	trappy
08 Haydock : Old Newton Cup	form
13 Newmarket: Bunbury Cup	trappy
15 York : John Smith's	neutral

AUGUST

02 Galway: Galway Plate	neutral
05 Goodwood: Stewards	form/statistics
23 York: Ebor	dark

SEPTEMBER

03 The Curragh: Cambridgeshire	form
06 Doncaster: Portland	form/statistics
16 Ayr: Gold Cup	neutral
20 Listowel: Kerry National	neutral
23 Ascot: Tote	possible
24 Ascot: Mile Final	trappy
24 Ascot: Showcase (Ritz)	dark

	30 Newmarket: Cambridgeshire	form/statistics
	30 The Curragh: Cesarewitch	form
OCTOBER		
	14 Newmarket: Cesarewitch	trappy
NOVEMBER		
	04 Doncaster: November	form/statistics
	11 Cheltenham: Thomas Pink	trappy
	25 Newbury : Hennessy	form/statistics
DECEMBER		
	02 Sandown: William Hill	neutral
	09 Cheltenham: Tripleprint Gold Cup	trappy
	27 Chepstow: Welsh National	form

2001

JANUARY

	22 Haydock: Peter Marsh	form/statistics
	27 Doncaster: Great Yorkshire Chase	form/statistics
FEBRUARY		
	03 Sandown: Tote	form/statistics
	10 Newbury: Tote Gold Trophy	form/statistics
	17 Newcastle: Tote Northern National	form/statistics
	24 Haydock: De Vere Gold Cup	trappy
	24 Kempton: Racing Post Chase	neutral
MARCH		
	Sandown: Imperial Cup	trappy

ALPHABETICAL ORDER, BY COURSE

AINTREE		
	Cordon Bleu	statistics
	Grand National	trappy
	John Hughes Memorial	statistics
	Red Rum	trappy
ASCOT		
	Mile Final	trappy
	Ritz	dark
	Tote	possible
	Victoria Cup possible	
AYR		
	Gold Cup	neutral
AYR (N.H.)		
	Scottish Grand National	trappy
CHELTENHAM: MARCH		
	Coral	trappy
	County	neutral
	Grand Annual	trappy
	Ladbroke	statistics
	Mildmay of Flete	statistics
	William Hill handicap chase	neutral
CHELTENHAM: OTHER		
	Thomas Pink Gold Cup	trappy
	Tripleprint Gold Cup	trappy
CHEPSTOW (N.H.)		
	Welsh National	form
CHESTER		
	Chester Cup	trappy
DONCASTER		
	Lincoln	trappy

November	form/statistics
Portland	form/statistics
DONCASTER (N.H.)	
Great Yorkshire Chase	form/statistics
FAIRYHOUSE (N.H.).	
Irish Grand National	trappy
GALWAY (N.H.)	
Galway Plate	neutral
GOODWOOD	
Stewards Cup	form/statistics
HAYDOCK	
Old Newton Cup	form
HAYDOCK (N.H.)	
Peter Marsh Chase	form/statistics
De Vere Gold Cup	trappy
KEMPTON (N.H.)	
Racing Post Chase	neutral
LISTOWEL (N.H.)	
Kerry National	neutral
NEWBURY (N.H.)	
Hennessy	form/statistics
Tote Gold Trophy	form/statistics
NEWCASTLE	
Northumberland Plate	trappy
NEWCASTLE (N.H.)	
Tote Northern National	form/statistics
NEWMARKET	
Any distance	form
Bunbury Cup	trappy
Cambridgeshire	form
Cesarewitch	trappy
ROYAL ASCOT	
Ascot stakes	trappy
Britannia	dark
Duke of Edinburgh	possible
King George V	statistics
Royal Hunt Cup	trappy
Wokingham	trappy
SANDOWN (N.H.)	
F Cup	trappy
Tote	form/statistics
Whitbread Gold Cup	trappy
William Hill handicap hurdle	neutral
THE CURRAGH	
7f+ handicaps	form
UTTOXETER (N.H.)	
Midlands Grand National	neutral
YORK	
Ebor	dark
John Smith's Cup	neutral

WINNING TYPES

DARK
Ascot: Ritz
Royal Ascot: Britannia
York: Ebor
FORM
Chepstow: Welsh National

Haydock: Old Newton Cup
Newmarket: any distance
Newmarket: Cambridgeshire
The Curragh: 7f+
FORM/STATISTICS
Doncaster: Great Yorkshire Chase
Doncaster: November
Doncaster: Portland
Goodwood: Stewards Cup
Haydock: Peter Marsh Chase
Newbury: Hennessy
Newbury: Tote Gold Trophy
Newcastle: Tote Northern National
Sandown: Tote
NEUTRAL
Ayr: Gold Cup
Cheltenham: County
Cheltenham: William Hill
Galway: Galway Plate
Kempton: Racing Post Chase
Listowel: Kerry National
Sandown: William Hill handicap hurdle
Uttoxeter: Midlands Grand National
York: John Smith's Cup
POSSIBLE
Ascot: Tote
Ascot: Victoria Cup
Royal Ascot: Duke of Edinburgh
STATISTICS
Aintree: Cordon Bleu
Aintree: John Hughes Memorial
Cheltenham: Ladbroke
Cheltenham: Mildmay of Flete
Royal Ascot: King George V
TRAPPY
Aintree: Grand National
Aintree: Red Rum
Ascot : Mile Final
Ayr : Scottish Grand National
Cheltenham: Coral
Cheltenham: Grand Annual
Cheltenham: Thomas Pink Gold Cup
Cheltenham: Tripleprint Gold Cup
Chester: Chester Cup
Doncaster: Lincoln
Fairyhouse: Irish Grand National
Haydock: De Vere Gold Cup
Newcastle: Northumberland Plate
Newmarket: Bunbury Cup
Newmarket: Cesarewitch
Royal Ascot: Ascot stakes
Royal Ascot: Royal Hunt Cup
Royal Ascot: Wokingham
Sandown: Imperial Cup
Sandown: Whitbread Gold Cup

NOTES

NOTES

NOTES